COMING

FORDHAM UNIVERSITY PRESS   NEW YORK 2017

COMING

JEAN-LUC NANCY
WITH ADÈLE VAN REETH

Translated by Charlotte Mandell

This book was originally published in French as Jean-Luc Nancy and Adèle Van Reeth, *La Jouissance*, Copyright © Plon, 2014.

The translation of "Nude Enumerated" also appears in *Two Lines* 25 (Fall 2016).

Fordham University Press has no responsibility for the persistence or accuracy of URLs for external or third-party Internet websites referred to in this publication and does not guarantee that any content on such websites is, or will remain, accurate or appropriate.

Fordham University Press also publishes its books in a variety of electronic formats. Some content that appears in print may not be available in electronic books.

Visit us online at www.fordhampress.com.

Library of Congress Cataloging-in-Publication Data available online at http://catalog.loc.gov.

Printed in the United States of America

19 18 17   5 4 3 2 1

First edition

CONTENTS

PREFACE TO THE ENGLISH-LANGUAGE EDITION

In French, the name of this book is *la Jouissance*. In English, *Coming*. In this way Charlotte Mandell solved the ever-renewed and strictly speaking impossible-to-solve difficulty posed by the translation of *jouissance*. This word designates the entire, limitless usage of a possession, with the twofold connotation of appropriation (or *consommation*, consumption) and pleasure carried to its height. (It stems from the Latin *gaudium*, joy, delight.) Hence its usage is divided into two distinct values: the legal meaning of complete ownership of a possession (one enjoys, *jouit de*, great wealth) or else the sensual meaning of a delectation or of voluptuousness—exclusively sexual voluptuousness following the usage that is dominant today in European French. The noun *jouissance* is thus used less to designate a state than the action or movement of *jouir*, enjoying—a verb that has also become mostly specialized in a sexual sense.

It is this duality, this ambivalence, even this duplicity, that also takes into account—in the most recent usages—the opposition between a consuming (or *"consumerist,"* as we say in English) *jouissance*, turned toward accumulation or absorption, and a *jouissance* that is on the contrary ecstatic, carried away, dis-appropriating. The first value is put into play in social theory; the second remains limited in discourse to sex and/or the mystical. But the mystical seems today to have been relegated to history and the word *jouissance* has acquired an almost exclusively sexual intensity.

In English, sexual orgasm is expressed by the verb "to come." This has no corresponding noun. What is shared by both lexical registers is an idea of accomplishment. In French, we say *venir* (to come) for "reaching *jouissance*," but the word is mostly used between sexual partners (*"viens!"* for example). In choosing the gerund "coming," Charlotte Mandell aptly brings out action or movement, *something that is in the process of occurring*, which, in fact, is attached to *jouissance* and to *jouir*: that is, precisely what remains irreducible either to a state or to an acquisition, to an accomplishment or to an appropriation.

It is to this irreducibility that we have devoted the dialogue that follows.

Jean-Luc Nancy

WHY SPEAK OF COMING (*JOUISSANCE*)?

You will find in this interview neither shrewd advice on how to have better orgasms (*mieux jouir*) nor despairing observations on a society that identifies sexual enjoyment (*jouissance*) with greedy absorption in property and pleasure. Nor will you find any claim to prove wrong those who have already thought about the vices and virtues of sexual fulfillment (*jouir*).

In the following discussion, we were guided by a shared curiosity and an interest that was as expected as it was incongruous. Expected, because it is not taboo for contemporary thinking to discuss sexuality (at least since Freud and Bataille, among others), and yet incongruous, because sexual pleasure (*jouissance*) is not the dominant motive for these thoughts, which consider the sexual relationship (*rapport*) without taking into account the actual *event* that coming (*jouir*) is. Expected again, because the word "*jouissance*" has come to designate less sexual pleasure than the apex of what has long been called consummation, understood as an appropriation of benefits and satisfactions. But incongruous, precisely because it will not be a matter so much of using this word with the stigmatization of an economy or an ideology, but of reassessing (*ressaisir*) this experience that acts like an individual and collective engine, and that has been by turns—or even simultaneously—praised and condemned.

We think that *jouissance* presents itself as a major motive for reflection. Although it has not been present as such on the philosophical scene for some time, it was so once, very openly, with Plato, as it was afterwards in less visible but no less powerful ways in reflections about love, passion, and pleasure—philosophical, mystical, poetic, and literary writings, to which we grant much importance in this interview. We have also chosen to confront head-on the political stakes entrained by sexual pleasure (*jouir*), whenever it becomes the subject both of public claims (come without any restrictions!) and of public condemnations.

What does the word *jouissance*, sexual pleasure, mean, then, what do we understand by it, what is implied by it? Perhaps something unheard-of, even unhearable. That is not a reason not to try to understand it, and that is what has led us to have this interview.

Adèle Van Reeth and Jean-Luc Nancy

COMING

Coming

PRELIMINARIES

ADÈLE VAN REETH: "*Jouissance*," pleasure: Now that is a difficult word to handle. It can mean satisfaction or excess, gluttony or voluptuousness . . . It's something of an indecent or suspicious word: It's embarrassing. It's almost impossible to handle.

JEAN-LUC NANCY: That's true, it doesn't make our task easy; either it has an obscene resonance, or it evokes greedy domination . . . But perhaps that's not by chance: If it makes us ill at ease, it's probably out of fear that it carries too much with it, it demands too much . . .

AVR: That at least is the situation today, when pleasure [*jouissance*] is associated with a sexual experience that people seek out or, on the contrary, that is frightening. Yet *jouissance*, etymologically, generally goes beyond the realm of sexuality.

JLN: Etymologically, there is no special relationship between the word *jouir* (from the Latin *gaudere*, "to rejoice") and sexuality. For a long time, *jouissance* has had a mainly legalistic sense, designating the effect of complete possession of something, a possession that allows a complete, limitless use of what I own: I am the owner of my pen, and if I want to destroy it, I can.

We are going to try to see how and why the first meaning of *jouissance* has gradually shifted over to the sexual meaning. I even have the impression that there is a twofold movement: first a veering toward the sexual, or sensual; then, more recently, an extension of the word toward consummation, in the name of a critique of the society of consumption. Today, *jouissance* is understood as consummation, but we forget that the end result of consummation [*consommation*] is consuming [*consumation*], hence the end of *jouissance*. I find it striking that *jouissance* is often understood in a critical, pejorative sense, and used about everything: Smart phones, for instance, are perceived as objects of pleasure [*jouissance*].

Then, we should remember that pleasure [*jouissance*] evokes two terms that belong to the same lexical field: on one hand, joy [*joie*]; on the other, rejoicing [*réjouissance*]. It even seems to me that these two terms have not always been distinguished: Think about the "joy" of the troubadour poets, which designates a joy of love that is indeed sensual, even sexual, but where precisely *jouissance* in the sense of consummation must be avoided.

One of the ordeals of courtly love even consisted of the knight sleeping with his lady without making love!

That is interesting: Joy can be thought of without *jouissance*. Today, joy has even become for us the opposite of *jouissance*: It elevates us, while *jouissance* is more corporeal, more earthly.

AVR: Joy might be de-sexed [*désexuée*], then, while *jouissance* might be sexual.

JLN: In a way, yes. De-sexed, very spiritual. The word "joy" almost summons the adjective "spiritual." In the language of today, when we say "what a joy to . . . ," it's very different from "what a pleasure!" If I say to someone: "The passage you wrote was truly for me a great joy," that is not the same thing as saying, "It was a pleasure to meet you."

AVR: Let's try to define the terms we'll need to discuss *jouissance*. How do you distinguish pleasure from joy?

JLN: It seems to me that pleasure corresponds more to what in Kant is called pleasant, to what relates to me as a subject: Pleasure pleases me [*le plaisir me plaît*], that is, it suits something inside me. Whereas joy carries me rather outside of myself, towards something else. To be even more precise, we must call on another word that we don't currently use: that of *beatitude*. In common use, "bliss" [*béat*] is a critical word, generally associated with optimism: We speak of blissful optimism. In reality, beatitude is the state of one who is blessed, or *beatus* in Latin. In the Catholic church, beatification designates the state previous to canonization. If I think of this word, it's because we find it in Spinoza, for whom joy occupies a very important place, starting from the basic difference between joyful passions and sad passions. Yet beatitude, in Spinoza, is first of all the state we reach when we are in the love of God, which for Spinoza is synonymous with intellectual love. Today, this term has become outmoded, almost ridiculous, but Spinoza defines it in the final proposition in his *Ethics* in a way I find truly admirable: "Beatitude is not the reward of virtue, but its very practice." Here we should not understand virtue in the moral sense, like total compliance with a certain moral demand. *Virtus* in Latin is the exercise of a force that is positive, the force of striving toward that love of God who is at the same time (since God, for Spinoza, is nature) the love of nature, the love of the world, of Being in general. With Spinoza, one can say that whereas pleasure is above all centripetal and appropriative, joy, on the other hand, is centrifugal and dis-appropriative, a disposition that is both active and striving towards something outside.

AVR: Would *jouissance*, then, be aligned with joy or beatitude?

JLN: From the perspective of Spinoza, I would say it's aligned with joy, since *jouissance* is a movement, an impulse [*élan*] and a passage, whereas beatitude (also called "felicity") designates a state, the state of knowledge of God or of the whole order of nature. It's the same as the difference between tension and accomplishment, or between movement and rest. That said, "virtue" also designates, in keeping with its Latin sense, active power, effort with something in view, as the last statement from the *Ethics* I cited signals. So it is also a desire, or an appetite: not desire for an object but the desire of "persevering in one's being," that is, going as far as possible in the act of existing. So beatitude is a state in which the desiring act is constantly renewed, re-launched. Spinoza notes that "we experience joy from it" by using the verb *gaudere* (from which "joy" and *jouissance* derive) and not *laetare* (whereas he first called joy *laetitia*, a more spiritual joy, less agitated or tumultuous).

We should note that Spinoza is far from praising sexual *jouissance*, but his thinking about the desire to be in an infinitely renewed impulse [*élan*] of correspondence with the infinite itself, with all the excess that one might find in it, has something remarkably sexual about it, although Spinoza himself does not note this.

AVR: You also mentioned the closeness between *jouissance* and rejoicing, *réjouissance*. How do you define rejoicing?

JLN: Rejoicing is not a term that's much used today, but it has often been associated with the public, the popular: I'm thinking of the expression of *réjouissances* *populaires*, popular festivities. The idea of festivities, *réjouissances*, refers to festive excess, to a certain suspension of everyday activities, but also to obligation and finality. That is where we find *jouissance*, in the sense of joyful acclamations greeting the arrival of an important person, like the *jouissance* of the people at the arrival of the king. I owe this to the poet Michel Deguy, who writes, "*Jouissance* is one of the rhetorical figures of acclamation at the arrival of someone. Come! Into the erotic poem I will entwine lines of thought."

AVR: Joy and *réjouissance*, then, are both on the side of excess, just like *jouissance*. Yet the evolution of the concept of *jouissance* can be observed as starting from the notion of appropriation: *jouissance*, pleasure, is no longer understood today as an aspect of property; one can enjoy something that one does not own. It is more on the side of expropriation.

JLN: That is probably when there is contradiction in the use of terms that may refer to a contradiction within the thing itself. You've just said that one does not own the thing one enjoys. But the law says exactly the opposite! The law stipulates that if it's a matter of an object, you are fully free to enjoy it. Freedom—in the sense of unbounded right—is implied by the idea of *jouissance*. So you can only do that if you are the owner of it. I don't have the right to do anything I like with your microphone, for example, because it's yours.

AVR: You do have the right! It's morality that forbids that, not the law.

JLN: Oh yes, it's the law! Because if I break your microphone . . .

AVR: I could sue you.

JLN: You could sue me. Whereas if I break this remote control that's next to me and that belongs to me, no one can sue me.

AVR: So *jouissance* understood in its legalistic sense defines the appropriation of an object and designates an owner, whereas non-legalistic *jouissance, jouissance* as experience, is not a matter of appropriation.

JLN: And to find out how the sense of the word—but also, I think, the thing—could lead in two different directions at once, we must question ourselves. For example, much has been spoken of possessing someone sexually. Today I have the impression it's less current, and poorly regarded. I'm sure one could easily find attestations, even literary ones, that would permit us to conceive of a form of possessing a woman that is not harmful for her, that would not lead her to be treated as a sexual object. But a woman can also "possess" a man; that is true also for a homosexual partner. These kinds of possessive relationships have been described (or written about) thousands of times. But if we so dislike using this term today, it's because we understand this possession, precisely, only as an appropriation, and because we belong to an era when possession can only be understood as possession of an object by a subject. Consequently, possessing a person comes down to making him or her into an object. You will note that we never speak of possessing a man (we don't speak of it often enough but that does not keep it from being possible, as I mentioned). I don't even know if the expression is present in the erotic love vocabulary of masculine homosexuality . . . On the other hand, it has often been said that a man could be possessed, but in the sense of diabolical possession, by a woman. We also speak of "taking." But "Take me!" is not necessarily a neurotic demand: There is a sense of capture and possession, of belonging, which is beyond legalistic, dominating appropriation. In "You belong to me," "I belong to you," what does this "to" mean? Is one being alienated? Devoted? Exposed?

In appropriation, we understand the root word "proper," in the sense of the property of something, as a proper noun. But what does *the property of someone* mean? The question comes up only starting from the instant you are in a subjective system. The property of a subject is this "itself" to which it is related. But this *itself* is never given as something; it is always distanced in a tricky, complex way. It escapes itself by joining itself. The relationship to self is a relationship to a relationship, to the relationship that is a "self" in itself. It is an infinite relationship. Where will you find the property of yourself? Where am I the same as me?

AVR: Without becoming an object for myself, since I am a subject.

JLN: From this point of view, it is important to be able to differentiate a subject on one hand from an object on the other that one appropriates. But if the subject has no relationship to itself, then to whom is the object appropriated? When I say that this pen is mine, I place myself in a very simple register, the legalistic register that stipulates that you do not have the right to take it from me. But who is me on the inside? Nothing at all, it's just a body that can hold this pen. And since this "me" cannot really be defined, it also tends to become another sort of object. So if we speak of sexual possession in a "proprietary" sense, one can say that the possessor objectifies himself as much as he objectifies the possessed. Understanding how a subject can become an object for someone else but also for him- (or her-) self, or else on the contrary not become that—that is decisive for the question of *jouissance* that concerns us.

ARE WE ALONE IN *JOUISSANCE*?

ADÈLE VAN REETH: *Jouissance* as experience implies a dissolution of the subject as well as the impossibility of appropriating its object. How then can we define what makes us enjoy [*jouir*]? And above all, since the question of object goes back to that of the subject: Who is it that enjoys [*jouit*]?

JEAN-LUC NANCY: It is because, in *jouissance*, these two questions of object and subject are linked, that *jouissance* can be in such a proximity not only with joy, but also with *réjouissance*, exuberance in general. Exuberance is a word marked by femininity: It is the swelling of the breast (*uber* in Latin), the milk that gushes forth. We can also think of ecstasy, a word of Heidegger's and Schelling's that signifies "being outside of oneself," or rather "*élan*, impetus, outside of oneself." In this outside-of-self, appropriation is impossible, because in it the subject is not a thing, a substance, but a simple punctual "I," which allows us to unify our representations. But this relationship no longer functions in *jouissance*, which implies rather that we abandon representation, and thus leave that "I" that can no longer accompany the experience of *jouissance*. I think that is really what we are talking about, that loss of a subject capable of saying "I."

AVR: Yet *jouissance*, far from being abstract, is always an experience, which means that it holds meaning only for a particular person. For instance, if we confine ourselves to sexual *jouissance*, the one who is coming *[jouit]* can say, "I'm coming . . ." Who is this "I," then, who comes?

JLN: This crucial question finds a privileged inscription in Sade, for whom the one who comes enters into a twofold relationship with destruction. First of all, the relationship of the one coming with the one with whom he or she comes is a relationship of possession pushed to the point of destruction; he is enjoying *[jouit]* the risk of opening a gaping chasm in the very place where what is causing him or her to come exists. But this relationship with destruction turns against the one coming himself, who can try to go as close as possible to his own death. In Sade, we find heroes who have themselves hanged in order to ejaculate, after asking their valets to cut the rope at just the right instant. It's in these sorts of situations that, often, the Sadean hero says, I am coming [*je jouis*]. That is: I am being carried away by *jouissance*. The exclamation is torn from him. Often some sort of blasphemy is added: "Fucking God!"—which also testifies to his being carried away.

AVR: But does this mean that *jouissance* is inseparable from pain? Here, the person who says "I am coming" says it simultaneously with the experience of pain.

JLN: Pain is always present in *jouissance*, tangentially or asymptotically. The extreme intensity becomes unbearable, and perhaps one comes precisely from being at the limit: there where the height of excitation is exceeded and is beaten back, only finally to fail.

The Sadean hero intensifies the ambivalence of that instant when he cries out "fuck! [*foutre*]," which means *baiser*, and which he uses as a kind of condemnation or insult for what he is in the process of doing or undergoing. Today, we don't say *foutre* much anymore, or else just to designate sperm (cum). The Sadean hero, though, says, "Fuck! In the name of God, I'm coming!"—It's a proclamation. We can find these proclamations in a number of erotic poems, in Apollinaire's *Poems to Lou* for instance, where they are addressed to the other: "You are coming!" We heard it, too, in the "come" [*viens*] of Deguy that we mentioned earlier. What's more, in English, *jouir* is to come, *venir*.

AVR: . . . which we don't hear in the French term of *jouissance*.

JLN: In fact, the term *jouissance* is difficult to translate in a certain number of languages. In English and German, there is no word that is in the same family. Either the register is sexual, or, more rarely, legalistic. In German, *Genuss* evokes more the idea of satisfaction. But being satisfied with something signifies having enough of it, which leads us to the opposite of *jouissance*. Of course, the possessive aspect of *jouissance* is also linked to the idea of satisfaction: I want to have enough of it. But what does "having enough of it" mean? That implies the idea of an objective measure, which can be that of my means: I possess so much money and I will be satisfied if I obtain everything this money allows me to possess. But can I have enough of something that has no measure? That makes no sense. If my desire is measureless, it will never have enough, it will never reach a threshold. That is what happens for *jouissance*: It occurs outside of any measure or any idea of a threshold. Which does not mean that it never terminates, but rather that it is very difficult to know what that stopping-point is made of.

I would even say that the property of *jouissance* is to be endlessly renewed. This is very striking in the case of aesthetic *jouissance*, which we find in works of art, and to which we will return. Why doesn't art stop, why do people continue to create? Because in art as in sexual *jouissance*, we never say we've had "enough" of it. This idea makes no sense. If people continue to create and *jouir*, it's because desire doesn't stop when it takes one particular form. Because there is a constantly renewed desire, the desire to make new forms arise, that is, to make a new sensibility perceptible [*sensible*]. And this new sensibility is desired and created not because we lack something, or out of a compulsion for repetition, but because what is desired is the renewing of meaning *as such*. What art testifies to, then, is our desire to make sense infinitely.

AVR: Do you think that *jouissance* expresses a desire for meaning? If that is the case, this desire must emanate from someone, thus presupposing a subject of *jouissance*. But you have insisted on the dissolution of the subject in *jouissance*. Isn't there a contradiction?

JLN: Unless we wonder if it's desire itself that is the subject. In the same way that it's language that speaks and makes us speak, it's desire that is the subject of our desire. This desire has no relationship to self: It is impulse. When Freud says, "Impulses are our myths, and our doctrine of impulses is our mythology"—an extraordinarily bold, even provocative statement—he is expressing something very important. Here, we should understand "myth" in the sense of fiction, that is that space where explanation becomes useless; but we should understand it also as *muthos*, uttered speech. It is Plato who defines myth as a lying fable, whereas in Homer *muthos* refers to speech. There can be *logos* only because at a certain point, *muthos* opened the way to it, with

Plato especially. What's more, Plato set about fabricating his own myth, which is called philosophy.

Let's return to Freud: What is an impulse? The term designates the fact of being unable to think of ourselves otherwise than as driven on by something, which you could call gods or material forces (you can choose your myth). Heidegger would say we are driven, set off by the very fact of being. Freud, however, does not tell us by what we are driven, but this movement is precisely what we find in *jouissance*.

AVR: Not only does *jouissance* have no precise subject, but might it be the sign of belonging to a community, something that surpasses the subject and makes us join with being? We are almost in the Kantian experience of the beautiful, which attests to a sense shared by everyone. *Jouissance* might be the locus for such a shared meaning, a common sensibility.

JLN: Exactly, because since I am not the owner of my *jouissance*, I still experience it in a way that I can actually *be* there where however I cannot *find* myself. It is not enough to say that the subject is lost in *jouissance*—rather it is as if the self is subjected to it, in the earlier sense of subject, the subject of a monarch. *Jouissance* is stronger than me, but this subjection I know comes from elsewhere. It comes to me from the other, from others. That is why there is no solitary *jouissance*. Already I can hear objections pouring forth: "Of course there are solitary *jouissances*, everyone talks about solitary pleasure!" But precisely, the pleasure in question is not in fact solitary, because it cannot take place unless the subject places himself in exteriority in relation to himself—this can take several forms. First of all, this relationship is always imaginary, fantasy-based. Then, procuring pleasure by oneself implies a splitting in two [*dédoublement*]. It's a little like the famous chiasmus of Merleau-Ponty: When I touch my hand, I am both the hand that touches and the hand that is touched, I am both inside and outside. And when I touch myself, I experience this self as being outside of myself. I *refer* [*rapporte*] back to myself. This experience raises a classic question: Do I have a body or am I my body? To this very pertinent question we must reply: both. Because when I say I *am* my body, I cannot disregard the fact that I also possess it; and when I say I *have* a body, I am forced to note of this body that . . . I *am* it. Having a body refers to the object, being a body refers to the subject. But I myself am object as subject. At least so long as I regard my body not just as a tool. If I touch my body, and if my body touches itself to give itself pleasure, it is outside of itself. That said, masturbation is not exactly the same thing as the sexual relationship, since, precisely, in masturbation the other is reduced to the state of a fantasy. Whereas in the sexual relationship the other is not based on fantasy—although a certain kind of psychoanalysis says there is no sexual relationship without fantasy . . .

AVR: But one can make love with someone while fantasizing that the person is different, even someone else. Isn't fantasy always present?

JLN: Probably, but that is always only a possibility, not a necessity. One day, a psychoanalyst told me there was necessarily fantasy in the sexual relationship. I retorted, "Oh no, that's disgusting!" He hit the roof. Actually, I think the body of the other is always there, in its exteriority and its singularity, as a body that is not my own. It is with the outside of this body that *jouissance* is shared. Shared in the sense that what I take pleasure from is just as much the pleasure of the other as my own.

In *The Unavowable Community*, Blanchot mentions the novella by Marguerite Duras, *The Malady of Death*. In this text, a woman agrees to sleep with a man for money. It's the man who asks to pay; the reader doesn't know why the woman agrees, if not perhaps to allow this man to attain a thing to which he has no access, that is, love or *jouissance*. In Duras's tale, we can never know if he attains this, but we do know the woman comes (*jouit*). Blanchot does not recount the passage that describes the woman in the process of having an orgasm (*jouir*), but the one of the man's gaze at the woman's *jouissance*. It is the startled gaze of someone who sees *jouissance* but can neither attain it nor participate in it. I don't know what Duras had in mind, but I note a coherence with other texts by her that seem to say that only the woman truly achieves *jouissance*—or else it is through the feminine that there is access to *jouissance* for a man or for a woman. Blanchot draws the conclusion that *jouissance* is necessarily solitary, even though it comes from a relationship with an other. He writes: "Pleasure, essentially, is what escapes." We can see a contradiction in this: If pleasure is what escapes, then *jouissance* is impossible. But I think that Blanchot means the opposite: Pleasure escapes, but it is in the escaping that there is pleasure. And that is where we find the other: Escaping outside of oneself sends us to the other, the one to whom I say "Come!" and who answers me.

I wonder if the dimension of shared meaning, which you mentioned in your question, might be a fundamental issue of *jouissance*, understood in the wider sense of the term, not exclusively in its sexual sense. Because the shared sense of sexual *jouissance* does not necessarily mean simultaneous *jouissance*, in the sense of orgasm. Perhaps we would have to rid ourselves of an overly orgasmic view of things, and wonder where sexuality begins and where it stops. Perhaps it begins very, very far from the sexual act itself.

AVR: The examples you've chosen evoke sexual *jouissance* more as an experience of a radical alterity than as the occurrence of a shared meaning. In the example from Marguerite Duras, as well as the reading Blanchot gives of it, the distinction between masculine and feminine *jouissance* seems to go without saying.

Lacan presents feminine *jouissance* as an experience of alterity in its most radical, hence most unfathomable, quality.

JLN: I don't think that what Lacan says about feminine *jouissance* means it's only the woman who *jouit*. If I were to rephrase it in my own words, I would say of feminine *jouissance* that it is neither the possession nor appropriation of something, but rather openness to an alterity, since the woman is in the position of what Lacan calls "the Other," the big Other. *Jouissance*, then, would make woman into that big Other, that is, that which remains outside of language and meaning, and which for that reason escapes any capture by a subject. Lacan says the same thing about the sexual relationship as such, whence his famous phrase: There is no sexual relationship. Masculine *jouissance* in this formulation is only something that has to do with desire for a satisfaction, itself illusory, to compensate for the lack of castration. This analysis can seem simplistic, but it is linked to an effort I find entirely praiseworthy: to try to find the *meaning* of *jouissance*, beyond the fulfillment of satisfaction, in a *sortie* outside oneself, into exuberance, ecstasy . . .

AVR: But why qualify this *jouissance* as "feminine" when we think of it as ecstasy? Why invoke gender to think of an experience that is both universal and singular?

JLN: Remember what Freud says: There is feminine and masculine in every individual, biologically and socially determined. We should not think of this co-existence of the masculine and feminine in each person as two chromosomes facing off against each other, but as an intertwining, as a complexity that is itself infinite.

AVR: What matters here is the presence of an alterity necessary to *jouissance*. You said that *jouissance* was never solitary. That when I come [*jouis*], and when I am beyond subject, I also come [*jouis*] from alterity, but who is this other? Either one or the other: Either it's the other in its most abstract dimension, like the idea I form of the other, or a fantasy; or it's the other as a body, who then becomes the instrument of my *jouissance*. We come back to appropriation. In both cases, the other is indeed indispensable to *jouissance*, but at the same time, he is barely involved . . . What I mean is that it seems to me that *jouissance* remains something solitary, that it is an experience irreducible to the other's; it is profoundly subjective, and that one cannot share. I cannot know if the one who is coming (possibly) with me is having the same experience as I am. It is an experience of isolation. Unshareable.

JLN: But in this isolation you do not find yourself alone with yourself. Because the experience also passes through speech, whether it's "come," or "I'm coming." And then there is the body of the other, about which you said it could become an instrument of pleasure [*jouissance*]. The instrument itself becomes something other, because the body of the other is mixed with my body. In the sexual relationship, a body is created that is aligned with Antonin Artaud's "organ-less body," that is, a body conceived no longer as an organism, but as the production of desire. Perhaps a twofold double body without individuals . . . without people . . . *Jouissance* carries this experience of alterity to this point, like an alterity of bodies that no longer conform to their functional organization. An entirely different functionality has moved in: We look at each other, but no longer in the same way, and very soon we no longer look at each other, we touch each other. Sometimes, one can be on the verge of being wounded. In the film *Trouble Every Day*, Claire Denis pushes the metaphor of a kiss as a bite to its very limit. The film begins with the image of the shoulder of a young woman, on which we see the trace of a bite. Later on, we realize she has just gotten married to a man who has come down with a disease that makes him cannibalistic, and that another woman (played by Béatrice Dalle) has transmitted the illness to him. We see him biting the young woman, then immediately moving away so as not to eat her, literally. Later on, we see Béatrice Dalle seducing another, younger boy. The boy feels pleasure [*jouit*] as she kisses him, caresses him, then he begins screaming when she bites him very deeply. She ends up devouring him. The kiss as bite exists; it is not just metaphorical. The erotic, loving caress can extend into scratching. Here we are touching a perilous extreme, since lovers can go so far as to desire to kill each other. This desire to share a desired or endured death is a background to most love stories, not just in the Western, Christian world. Some Chinese, Japanese, and even Quechua legends recount this shared death of lovers. Thus, Messiaen adapted a Quechua legend in which both lovers share death, for his ensemble of musical pieces called *Harawi*. It is not a question of cannibalism, but of a desire to enter death together, that is, to pass into the absolute outside [*le dehors absolu*]. That is why the fantasy of a *jouissance* that is absolute satisfaction is dangerous, since that is a deadly, fatal *jouissance*. But that is just the opposite of what *jouir* means!

In this desire to share death, we find the idea of community, but also that of isolation that you were mentioning. Because in death one will surely be as completely reunited as separated, including from oneself. So I would say that *jouissance* is solitary insofar as I am also separated from myself. It is a solitude that is extremely difficult to capture, a solitude in relation to everything, subject or object, hence in relation to isolation itself . . . an *absolitude*, if I may say so.

AVR: How do you understand Lacan's phrase asserting there is no sexual relationship? If there is no sexual relationship, there is no sexual *jouissance*. But wouldn't it be truer to understand not that *jouissance* is impossible, but that it is inconceivable? Just as the fact that there is no sexual relationship would signify that there is no thinkable relationship. It would be a way to preserve the space unique to *jouissance* as experience.

JLN: That is probably what Lacan means. "There is no sexual relationship" can be understood in several ways: There is no proportion, no commensurability, no conclusion either. The sexual relationship cannot be written down. The implication is: There is no account of it, no "report" [*rapport*, which also means "relationship"]. But it is precisely to that extent that there is a real *rapport*, which demands incommensurability and a form of non-conclusion. A relationship is maintained [*s'entretient*]. It is not completed. A completed, accomplished relationship is either a breakup, or a fusion. And in fusion there is no longer any relationship. It would be truer to say, then, that *jouissance* is inconceivable, not impossible.

The Impossible is the title of a book by Bataille, in which eroticism is caught in an internal, sometimes contradictionary, tension, insofar as for him, true desire is that of fusing, which never happens. He concludes: "Eroticism is a comedy," just as he concludes, "Sacrifice is a comedy." This is the congenital sin of Bataille: He is too Catholic, he has too much of a need to think of a constant transgression. (But we will go back to that, it's always a way to feel the intensity unique to a certain Christian *jouissance* or joy . . .) He ends up not seeing that if fusion had taken place, there would be nothing left to fuse, there would be no more desire. But he has a keen sense of excess, of the infinity of desire.

If we follow this necessity for distance [*écart*] within the relationship itself—that is, within desire—to the end, we must admit that when distance vanishes tendentially into *jouissance*, then there is nothing more to take, nothing more to feel. Everything escapes. That is also the point when one comes [*jouit*]. But that solitude is solitude in the inconceivable. Or in the unattainable: Can one manage to be "alone" except in an "absolitude" that would mean "solitude absolutely exposed to the other solitude"? Bataille also says we attain, or accede to (*nous accédons*), and that what we attain conceals itself (*se dérobe*). But we accede to that which is without access.

FROM ANIMAL INSTINCT
TO DESIRE OF THE OTHER

How to Go from Plaisir *to* Jouir*?*

ADÈLE VAN REETH: The ambivalence of *jouissance* is fascinating. The experience of alterity is at the source of *jouissance*, including alterity to self in the case of masturbation; yet at the same time, *jouissance* is unshareable. In his *Critique of Judgment*, Kant explains how, when I deem a work of art or a landscape beautiful, immediately I postulate a universality of my judgment: It is inconceivable to me that anyone could not find this sunset beautiful. But I cannot share this experience of the beautiful, just as I cannot convince someone of the beauty of a sunset if he is not responsive to it. I can simply postulate, wager that everyone can experience the beautiful, and thus that there exists a kind of meaning that is common to all humans. The same is true for *jouissance*, which is a singular experience that I cannot imagine not being shared. Does this mean that there is an aesthetic dimension to *jouissance*?

JEAN-LUC NANCY: Freud explicitly establishes the transfer of aesthetic *jouissance* to sexual *jouissance*. He even goes so far as to explain one by means of the other, and in both senses: once in *Jokes and Their Relation to the Unconscious* and another time in his *Three Essays on the Theory of Sexuality*, two books he wrote at the same time, on two desks. In each of the books a note says, "on this point, I have explained myself in the other book," which is amusing but also revealing: for "this point" is that of pleasure as tension . . .

Let's start with the sexual aspect. After having spoken of infantile sexuality and the oral, anal, and genital stages, Freud analyzes the sexual relationship as a relationship of seduction. Curiously, without saying so, he follows an obvious order of parsing: He says the relationship begins by gazing, then by hearing, then by touching, which allows him to describe the erogenous zones, and to say that the entire body can be an erogenous zone. Only then does he come to the genitalia. In this trajectory, Freud does not point it out, but we again find ourselves within the stage-by-stage analysis of sexual maturation, and Freud points out that stopping at one of these stages in the progression of seduction is perversion. By perversion, he does not mean to designate a pathology, but a deviation in relation to the goal, which is genital. For me, that is an initial weakness of Freud's: He remains within a teleology, as if there were a procedure to follow, one that should end in a certain way. A tension that is supposed to be released.

But at that instant Freud poses this question: How can we comprehend that what is within tension procures pleasure? Lacan would take up this idea in the form of a paradox. Freud replies: Pleasure occurs because the subject knows that the tension will resolve itself into final satisfaction. This affirmation seems to me to pose a problem, again. In *Jokes and Their Relation to the Unconscious*, Freud explains that the joke—which serves him as an aesthetic model—procures pleasure by allowing an impulsive discharge to take an agreeable form. It consists of the conjunction between something pleasant and the meaning it conveys (which is not pleasant in itself). But Freud does not really explain this link between pleasure and tension. He fails to see, first of all from the aesthetic point of view, that the tension that corresponds to the production of form, the aesthetic gesture (think of the gesture of someone drawing) is a pleasure in itself—it is the pleasure of desire. Desire pleases itself. But to understand this, we must precisely not think of desire in an exclusively teleological way— that is, striving toward an object, a result—but rather— and here I'm returning to Spinoza—as *conatus*, as effort, impulse, which is also to say as *virtus*, "force." When Spinoza speaks of "persevering in one's being," what being is he talking about? This being is existing. It is not the persevering in his being of someone sitting in his armchair who can no longer move from it. It is this uniquely aesthetic pleasure of being within tension, the effort of a form in the process of being made, and which, in a way, must never be completed. What we enjoy in an aesthetic form is the movement of this form, even though it then ends up being completed. What's more, an aesthetic form is probably never exhausted and, on the contrary, does not stop enjoying itself (*jouir d'elle-même*).

AVR: So just as there is no formula for the beautiful, insofar as the beautiful is not reducible to a collection of elements, colors and forms, so is *jouissance* not the outcome of a path to be followed, whether sexually or aesthetically. In both cases, from *plaisir* to *jouir*, there is a leap that is of a qualitative order, meaning that the passage from *plaisir* to *jouir* is neither necessary nor obvious. It is not enough to have a lot of *plaisir* in order to *jouir* . . .

JLN: Of course. Think of erotic art, which comes from the desire to come "well" [*"bien" jouir*], and which, when it becomes the subject of discourse, wavers between advice for those who don't know how to go about it and the so-called infallible formula. What's more there is a model, the Kama-Sutra, which is very poorly understood by Westerners, because it wasn't made in order to teach people how to make love well; it is part of a religious practice. This model is connected to the practice of a sexual relationship with no orgasm. This is aesthetic *jouissance*, like the *jouissance* of form in its formation. In *La Formation des formes*, Juan Manuel Garrido, a young Chilean philosopher, asks how Kant's *a priori* forms are produced. This questioning opens onto a very wide space of thinking, a reflection about form as what forms *itself* [*se* forme], rather than as what *gets* formed [*est* formé]. His text is responding to the definition of form by Focillon, in *The Life of Forms in Art*: "A sign signifies an object, form signifies only *itself*."[1] This sentence is heavy with meaning. Because to signify itself is precisely to leave the register of the sign.

We could say that the subject of *jouissance* is one that only signifies itself. Or even that it's *jouissance* that signifies itself, hence is a sort of pure form, but with the difference that in sexual *jouissance*, there are no longer distinct forms—neither visual nor aural, not even tactile . . .

AVR: While the characteristic of aesthetics is to play with form or forms, in sexual *jouissance*, there is a de-formation of all form.

JLN: That's what I meant in speaking about bodies. In *jouissance*, they become almost formless. Which is radically opposed to that call to eroticism, in advertising or movies, always summoning beautiful, perfected forms. Whereas in eroticism, in *eros*, these forms become undone.

AVR: Which brings us back to the relationship between *jouissance* and the death wish, the impulse toward destruction.

JLN: Yes, there is destruction, even without the shadow of a bite, since in any case we don't really look at the body in front of us, it's not the form of the other that matters. But this "destruction" produces something else, it does not necessarily lead to death. There is a leap beyond the universe of forms; that's why there can be a lot of desire and erotic force with someone who is not "hot."[2] And this, to my knowledge, has been understood only by David Hume. He writes: "The beauty of a person comes from his feeling of being desired." That is wonderful! It's extraordinary.

AVR: That's true . . . As if a person's beauty came from the feeling, or even the certainty, that he or she arouses desire.

JLN: The day I read that sentence I understood how to pass beyond the power of supposedly erotic beauties in images, texts, pornography. Eroticism or pornography are two systems of accepted, defined forms. But in the act of the relationship [*rapport*], forms are invented—and they even invent their own excess, their own surpassing.

But let's go back to Freud. For him, aesthetic form serves only as a vehicle for the release of a drive. Which makes aesthetic form remain always pending [*en souf-*

france]. From the sexual perspective, anything that corresponds to aesthetic forms also disappears, but forms had a usefulness, that of arriving at the genital stage, which is dominated by what Freud calls *Entladung*, that is, discharge. The example here is first of all masculine, since masculine discharge is the most visible. For Freud, that is the culmination, the moment when tension disappears. What interests him is this need of a tension to lead us to discharge. We could object: Why do we create tension only to discharge it? Freud would probably reply that tension is not created, that it is already there . . . The question is, What is the purpose of drives: Does their meaning consist of lying in wait for their own resolution?

AVR: Unless we see in a drive the best way to continue to desire, since every satisfaction is only ephemeral. Since *jouissance* is made of pleasure, it is necessarily conditioned by time. That's what makes it fascinating: on one hand, ecstasy, which surpasses all bounds and all known pleasure; on the other, the endless desire to return to it, hence dissatisfaction *par excellence*.

JLN: The links between pleasure and satisfaction are complex. And pleasure has several meanings. Take the term "excitation." *Exciter*, in Latin, means to call on someone to come out, to call outside. This is not the case in pleasure in its current use. Plato shows that pleasure does not come only from the satisfaction of a need. He explains: If I am thirsty, I can drink until I quench my thirst, and when I'm no longer thirsty, I'll be satisfied. There we have a very simple satisfaction, which means I do not need to drink anymore. But if I continue to drink, it's because I'm looking for something else, the pleasure of drinking in order to drink. And that is why the drinker drinks. What does that mean? That in humans, you can never distinguish clearly between need and desire. Of course there are elementary needs, and the thirst of someone in the desert and that of someone next to a glass of water are not the same. But I think that in present situations we all feel that to the satisfaction of need, to the alleviation of dryness in the mouth, is also joined that additional thing, which is the coolness of water, the taste of this water . . . Let's stick to the example of water, which is close to need. Why, for example, can one prefer fizzy water, even when one is very thirsty? Because the sparkle of the bubbles produces a kind of excitation. Which explains the invention of bubbles. Or of champagne. And it's champagne Freud is thinking of, in a letter to Marie Bonaparte, when he speaks of his dog and says, How happy, how calm this dog is! She doesn't ask any questions . . . It's on that occasion that he writes that as soon as one poses a question to oneself about the meaning of life, one is a little sick. And I'm thinking, he says, of Don Juan's champagne aria. Freud is almost in the process of *jouir* in this passage of the letter; he is enjoying the animality beside him and he is evoking the hero who is a *jouisseur par excellence*.

AVR: Bubbles are a luxury insofar as they are not necessary. They're something superfluous, which bring an additional amount of pleasure. So *jouissance* might be both something uniquely animal, insofar as it corresponds to an irrepressible desire that can drive one to the point of wanting to devour the other, and also an absolute luxury characteristic of humanity. Isn't *jouir* the pleasure of having pleasure?

JLN: The pleasure of having pleasure . . . it's absolutely that! Sartre says, "There is no pleasure that does not know itself as pleasure." We could say the same thing the other way around: There is no pain that does not know itself as pain. Pleasure is a state that seeks out its own perpetuation, while pain seeks out its own cessation, but it's exactly the same thing in each sense. Aside from that aspect you already mentioned earlier, where *jouissance* can be suffering, precisely because you arrive at a limit that you can only surpass, to be on the side of excess which can become unbearable, which always becomes a little unbearable, or comes close to that. We can understand this excessiveness better by the extremity of pain, where it seemed sometimes to grasp, very briefly, its closeness to pleasure, in a moment of time. Something that would respond to the twofold value of what we call "provocation" or "irritation" [*"agacement" ou "irritation"*].

AVR: In the beginning of *Sodome et Gomorrhe* [*Cities of the Plain*], Proust's narrator listens without their knowledge to the Baron de Charlus and Jupien indulging in extremely noisy sexual pleasures. He compares the cries he hears to those of a man having his throat slit, and concludes that "if there is one thing as loud as suffering, it's pleasure." Might pain and pleasure have a certain intensity in common?

JLN: A very strong pain always has something shrill about it. Pleasure too. In a way, this pleasure or this pain are lost in the acuity of a point, which by definition has no dimensions, and it's in this point that the body goes out of itself. Sometimes, the entire body comes, and one comes to yearn for the disappearance of this expanse of body, as in death.

AVR: One could, on the contrary, see it as a leap of life within a body that's suffering or coming. And *jouissance* can engender more life, or even another life: In some cases, the sexual relationship results in procreation . . .

JLN: For me, that's a completely open question. On one hand one can say that humanity has always perceived sexual *jouissance* in its exceptional, exorbitant, exuberant nature, in a multiplicity of ways, procreative or not. Think of the different forms of sacralization of sexuality, from the sacred prostitutes of Babylon to Hinduism. Think of virginity, of excision. Everything isn't always linked solely to procreation. But in our culture, people have thought that sexual pleasure was, at bottom, nature's way to lead people to reproduce. Kant, however, is not content with this explanation, and writes, in a note to his *Anthropology*, that when the philosopher considers the system of sexuality, he can only remain stymied before an abyss, because he does not understand why nature chose something so complicated for reproduction.

Today, we've gone over to the other side. We think that sexuality is in itself—and I would say in law as well—completely independent of reproduction, and thus that sexual pleasure seeks itself for its own sake. People have always known how to seek out sexual pleasure for itself, even though it has long inevitably been linked to reproduction. The technological research into the control of reproduction is much older than we think, but it was never really effective until the arrival of the pill. Then began a period during which sexuality was freed from the constant fear of pregnancy, a free sexuality. But AIDS put an end to what's been called "the enchanted interval" [*la parenthèse enchantée*].

Sexual pleasure with its exorbitant quality, linked to *jouissance*, has always been present. How, then, can we think of the child? We could wonder if the child is a *jouissance*, but one placed inside an other. Or as an other. For at bottom, why do we make children? It's obvious we make children for ourselves. Because in the desire for a child, it's a certain form of alterity that is desired, an alterity attached to self, but that one desires as being detached from self.

AVR: That's just how we've described the experience of *jouissance*!

JLN: In fact, having a child is experiencing self as being outside of self, and this outside-of-self is itself someone else. It's an experience in which we find the question of *souffrance* in *jouissance*—a *souffrance* that remains bounded by time, whereas the child is essentially the one who leaves, just as pleasure is essentially that which escapes.[3] But the child who has left becomes "himself" and that is a joy. The child might be this alterity incarnate, who is truly an other but an other to whom the desire of *jouissance* has led, and who has carried *jouissance* off with him . . .

AVR: . . . or prolonged it. By giving it a *durée* that is not just that of the moment of the act, of orgasm, but that of an entire life.

JLN: Which will become his own *jouissance*. It's always a very important role, in all societies, that of reaching puberty, with the possibility of *jouissance*. Today, in our society, there's no longer really an initiation; sexuality arrives at an increasingly early age. Many parents wonder if their child has "already slept" with someone . . . In this we can see curiosity, anxiety, but also a kind of voyeurism, an expression of a desire to reclaim some of the *jouissance* that was carried away by the child. And the older the child gets, the further the adult grows from the possibility of making children.

And even from *jouir*—at least in the most immediate sense.

This feeling does not contradict the idea that it's the species that reproduces. All species reproduce. But humanity makes love at any time. True, Bonobo apes are familiar with masturbation, sodomy, homosexuality . . . but they do not have the prohibition of incest. Among humans, this interdiction does not prevent a huge number of actual instances of incest from taking place, but they are transgressions. But incest is linked to exogamy, to the opening up of kinship. What's more we don't find, or else find very rarely, among humans the arousal of sexual desire linked to periods of fertility.

Of course, biological reproduction has its marks: Children bear the characteristics of the parents. But biological reproduction has, among humans, a very weak reality. It is social and psychological reproduction that are important. I imagine that those are my children, and in a sense, that is the determining thing: They become largely the children one has represented as being one's own.

Thus the relationship of *jouissance* to the child is real, and it is not simply a relationship instrumentalizing the desire to *jouir* in order to lead humans to reproduce. Which explains very well how a homosexual couple can want children which it cannot create but which will still be a *jouissance* . . .

TOWARD INFINITY AND BEYOND

Is There an Art to Jouir?

ADÈLE VAN REETH: *Jouissance* is an extremely fertile experience. Beyond procreation, the creative power of *jouissance* is expressed in the very gesture of the creator, as is the case in art. From the dissolution of the subject to the overflowing of pleasure, what is the point in common between sexual and aesthetic *jouissance*?

JEAN-LUC NANCY: Perhaps every work of art is in a way a direct or indirect inscription of *jouissance*, and surely not by sublimation. Psychoanalysts say today that sublimation is a feeble concept of Freud's. In fact, it's not a question of a "spiritualization" of desire, but rather of another investment of sexual energy. Vasari relates how when the painter Raphael was working for a prince he regularly left his work to meet his mistress.

The prince had enough of this and ordered that the mistress be sent for with all her servants and that they come to his palace. He set her up in an apartment so that Raphael could have her within reach . . . It's this passage in Vasari that caused Nietzsche to say, "Without an enormous quantity of sexual energy, a Raphael would not be possible," which is surprising, since sexuality was not Nietzsche's strong point. So there's no need to be a sexual superman to have a good idea of what's going on . . .

What both art and sexuality absolutely have in common is a relationship to infinity. In the sense of good infinity, as Hegel calls it, actual infinity, immeasurable infinity. Hence questions like "Why do people continue making art?" and "Why do we keep making love?" both have the same answer, which lies in the projection of an unyielding, eternal infinity, an image of eternity that is not mere perpetuity. People in the Middle Ages knew very well how to tell the eternal from the sempiternal: Eternity is not endless; it is outside of time. So it resembles the instant more than it does the eternal. *Jouissance* is truly in the instant, even though it's an instant that lasts for a little while . . . Just like the blink of an eye that, for Husserl, is an instantaneity—whereas for Derrida it has a *durée*, and it's from that *durée* of the blink of an eye that he draws *différance* (and not *différence*). But *différance* is precisely the relationship to self as that which differs from self. I would say rather: *Différance* is *jouissance*, and vice-versa. In *jouissance* I stray from myself in such a way that I am sent back to a self beyond any possible identity. In this instant the question of relationship to self is at play: Who am I, who is asking this question? This question is that of the writer, the artist, which makes all the discussions on the autonomous vs. biographical nature of the work completely pointless, since if the work of art is always the work of an artist, it is still not the expression of a personality. The work makes itself [*se fait*], it has or it is its own "self," it does not express another self—but it can cause one either to *jouir* or to *souffrir*.

This desire to go out of oneself will be music for one person, color for another. In both cases, something shows us that what we desire most strongly is to depart, to go out.

AVR: Let's take an example: *Sexus*, by Henry Miller. From the writing in this text emanates a twofold, infinite power of overflowing [*débordement*]: on one hand, sexuality; on the other, writing. Both are caught in the same impulse [*élan*] of excess, like one single creative power. What's more, the narrator is constantly in movement; he paces up and down the streets wondering why he isn't writing. In the meantime, he *jouit* . . . as in this text:

It was a warm night and I lay back full length looking up at the stars. A woman passed but didn't notice me lying there. My cock was hanging out and beginning to stir again with the warm breeze. By the time

Mara returned it was quivering and jumping. She kneeled beside me with the bandages and the iodine. My cock was staring her in the face. She bent over and gobbled it greedily. I pushed the things aside and pulled her over me. When I had shot my bolt she kept right on coming, one orgasm after another, until I thought it would never stop.

We lay back and rested a while in the warm breeze. After a while she sat up and applied the iodine. We lit our cigarettes and sat there talking quietly. Finally we decided to go. I walked her to the door of her home and as we stood there embracing one another she grabbed me impulsively and whisked me off. "I can't let you go yet," she said. And with that she flung herself on me, kissing me passionately and reaching into my fly with murderous accuracy. This time we didn't bother to look for a vacant patch of ground, but collapsed right on the sidewalk under a big tree. The sidewalk wasn't too comfortable—I had to pull out and move over a few feet where there was a bit of soft earth. There was a little puddle near her elbow and I was for taking it out again and moving over another inch or so, but when I tried to draw it out she got frantic. "Don't ever take it out again," she begged, "it drives me crazy. Fuck me, fuck me!" I held out on her a long while. As before, she came again and again, squealing and grunting like a stuck pig. Her mouth seemed to have grown bigger, wider, utterly lascivious; her eyes were turning over, as if she were going into an epileptic fit. I took it out a moment to cool it off. She put her hand in the puddle beside her and sprinkled a few drops of water over it. That felt marvelous. The next moment she was on her hands and knees, begging me to give it to her assways. I got behind her on all fours; she reached her hand under and grabbing my cock she slipped it in. It went right to the womb. She gave a little groan of pain and pleasure mixed.[1]

JLN: Note the use of a crude, vulgar, at times ironic vocabulary, bordering on the pornographic—the pornographic consisting of showing directly that thing that neither should nor could be shown. In pornographic films, the embarrassing thing stems from the fact that the film feels so compelled to show the various genitalia that it all becomes incoherent or improbable. The sole aim becomes showing whether or not a penis is entering the other. Miller, on the contrary, puts in place an alternation between these obscene words and the rest of the scene, the cat, the woman passing, the grass, the details on the sidewalk . . . which makes the reader not feel summoned to a sort of voyeurish precipitation. All Miller's art consists in arranging things so that the reader is always inside the movement of description, that something else is happening other than their fucking, even when that's all that's being described!

AVR: The background is very ordinary: a sidewalk, a garage, the cat, the tree . . . But it's the background that receives the experience of pleasure [*jouissance*], that limitless power that is described with humor and obscenity. The beauty of this passage comes from the contrast between the two, including with the female character who keeps coming, orgasm after orgasm. We find the infinite here that had led us to Miller, this going outside of oneself by repetition. Here we see the opposite of satisfaction as Freud understood it.

JLN: And the female character says, "I don't care if it hurts." One phrase holds my attention: "utterly lascivious," translated as *lascive dans toute la force du terme*. *Lascivious* is a strong word, in both French and English, in its sonority: this "sc" that mixes two kinds of sibilants has something sinuous, serpentine, intertwined about it. I hear in it both entwining and abandon, satisfaction in tasting pleasure. It's the pleasure of taking pleasure . . . I'm also struck by this phrase: "*jusqu'à la matrice, recta*," for "it went right in to the womb." "*Recta*" evokes, in an exclamation, the blow that hits the nail on the head. And the womb, the *matrice*, designates the back of the vagina, which is the uterus or the womb. There is something very strong about this word "*matrice*," "womb," which evokes childbirth. It's amusing to note that Miller uses a word evoking maternity to designate an anatomic reality. The terms *matrice* and *recta* are incongruous, and don't normally have a place in a purely erotic or strictly anatomical register. *Matrice* . . . like *lascif*, lascivious, the word has a certain effect . . . I would call it "acid" . . .

AVR: These terms have a poetic richness about them. They send us back to the very gesture of writing, the verbal gesture that provokes the overflowing of self and sense through words. For while this text is very sexual, the *jouissance* of the writer (and of the reader) is also of another order. What is the difference between purely sexual *jouissance* and aesthetic *jouissance*?

JLN: I'll insist: This difference is not on the order of sublimation. What the artistic gesture and the sexual gesture have in common is the traversing [*traversée*] of the subject: *jouissance* emerges from behind me and goes beyond me. That is why we always have as many reasons to deny that an individual is the author of his work as we have to attribute it to him; because, in a way, what he creates *passes through* him. A great artist let himself be traversed by a desire. Matisse said that one must always obey the desire of the line. It is the line that desires, not Monsieur Matisse. It is a line, a sonority, a melody, the color of a rhythm that takes hold of someone. The painter Simon Hantaï insisted on the fact that the artist, in this instance Hantaï himself, was nothing at all; he would go down on all fours and spread out his painting. One day, I told him I could do the same thing. "Oh no, no, no!" he replied. "Whyever not?" "Because it's me!" Paradox? No, because in his work, he's the one who does everything, and the slightest gesture is his gesture—and there's nothing "subjective" about that. What sexual and aesthetic *jouissance* have in common, then, is an incredibly strong investment of singularity, and something that, through this singularity, surpasses it and carries it elsewhere. But the main difference between the two is that on the aesthetic side a work is produced that is more comparable to a child than to sexual *jouissance*, insofar as something outside of, external to, the self is produced. The artist is in action in his work, and he also takes pleasure [*jouit*] from being in the process of working. He suffers too, it's always laborious. In painting for example, he must always come back from outlining the form itself to preparing the colors, the tools, the canvas . . . His work is external to him, the body passes outside, whereas sexual *jouissance* is without an oeuvre—unless there's impregnation, but that's another matter. It is not a form, but a transformation, performation, deformation of forms, of all perceptible forms and fashions [*façons*]. Think of the expression "to make love": When we make love, we do not produce something outside ourselves. As to what we actually make . . . "*Faire*" also has an obscene meaning.[2]

Faire is much in question in all this: *faire l'amour* (make love), *faire jouir* (make someone come), *faire un enfant* (make a child). . . . We're in a register of effectiveness, of full reality, of action and presence.

What is fascinating is this isolated kernel that I would call sex rather than sexuality. To speak of sexuality is to imply a function that's more or less unique to humans. Whereas sex designates nothing but the difference between the sexes, or the difference within sex. In the '70s they even spoke of "sexion." You know that some linguists tried to derive "*sex*" from *secare* (to cut)—but that doesn't work . . . But the word "sex" does signify a division. In Plato's *Symposium*, Aristophanes describes human beings as originally divided into three categories: male, female, and androgynous. All of them are spheres with four hands, four legs, and two faces on one head. They are so powerful that they want to take the place of the gods. To punish them for their pride, Zeus cuts them in half, then asks Apollo to sew up the stomach on the side of the cut. That's the navel. The sexual organs remain on the other side. Thus separated from their half, the men kept embracing themselves, nostalgic for their original union, letting themselves die of hunger. Zeus, not desiring the end of humanity, then decides to place the sexual organs on the front of the body, thus making coupling possible, and begetting by a man and a woman. Thus, the androgynous halves could ensure the lineage of humanity, while men who loved men allowed not life to be born, but spirit.

This myth allows us to think of the act of *jouissance* as a desire to emerge from self and to go toward the other to overcome division. Making division the condition for *jouissance* is to think of *jouissance* as the desire to overcome separation or traverse it, experience it— not annul it.

AVR: Except in the case of the artist, for whom work requires a certain solitude.

JLN: Yes, but the artist always creates for an other: a spectator, a reader, a listener. Duchamp showed the necessity of this gesture very well: He took a urinal, made it into a fountain, and presented it as a work of art. Duchamp's work is dependent on a gesture of presentation, which itself would be nothing without what he calls the *rendez-vous*. The artist, in presenting his work, arranges a meeting [*donne rendez-vous*] with the spectator after having had a meeting with the object itself. Which signifies that the "ready-made" does not consist of doing anything at all to an ordinary object; otherwise the meeting would never take place. The meeting is both making [*faire*] and letting come [*laisser venir*].

But for many artists, even when this meeting has taken place and produces a *jouissance* in the spectator, there remains a constantly renewed dissatisfaction that leads them to work again and again, to try other ways, without ever attaining satisfaction, even temporary satisfaction. In painting, I'm thinking of Cézanne. Sometimes, as in music, in Lachenmann for example, this dissatisfaction can engender a fury [*acharnement*] that ends up destroying even the possibility of the work. To overcome separation is, in fact, to renew it, to intensify it.

AVR: In his *Letters to a Young Poet,* Rilke gives advice to a young man who wants to become a writer. Among the letters he writes, which are for the most part extraordinarily beautiful, one of them asserts that writing and sexuality are the same pleasure [*jouissance*]. He is replying to his correspondent, who has asked his opinion about the work of the poet Richard Dehmel, and Rilke writes thus:

> Viarregio, near Pisa (Italy),
> April 13th, 1903.
>
> Richard Dehmel: His books affect me (and, incidentally, so does the man whom I know casually) in such a manner that when I have found one of his beautiful pages I am always afraid of the next, which may upset everything again and turn what is attractive into something unworthy. You characterized him very well with the term: "living and writing in heat."—*And* in fact artistic experience lies so incredibly close to that of sex, to its pain and its ecstasy, that the two manifestations are indeed but different forms of one and the same yearning and delight. And if instead of heat one might say—sex, sex in the great, broad, clean sense, free of any insinuation of ecclesiastic error, then his art would be very grand and infinitely important. His poetic power is great, strong as a primitive instinct; it has its own unyielding rhythms in itself and breaks out of him as out of mountains.[3]

This complete identification of sex with desire, including the desire to write, is fascinating.

JLN: When Rilke calls for the use of "sex" in the place of "heat," or desire, he means that often, the term "desire" is a euphemism, especially in his time. But desire signifies sexual desire, hence sex. Rilke conceives of the work of the writer as consisting, among other things, of calling things by their name, and he wants to revive the carnality evoked by the word "sex." That's what Miller would go on to do, he who was systematically opposed to the euphemization of sex. Remember the puddle of water in which Mara dips her finger to sprinkle the narrator's penis, which allows him to cool down a bit in order to go at it again. The liquefaction of the body in sex is fundamental—if I may say so—since that is what leads us to the formless, to that which loses its form. Many myths and representations grant a special role to liquid, like the foam from which Aphrodite is born. Elsewhere Miller also uses this expression: "Soaked like a sweating horse" . . . The liquid of discharge does not calm the tension, or not that alone, but it's the stream, the gush of fluid that perpetuates itself.

Rilke also speaks of writing as working toward the unknown, without goal. The same is true for a painter or a musician. Which does not exclude the presence of a *projet* (plan)—I use the word even though Bataille despised it. One can have a *"pro-jet"* but afterwards, it's *le jet*, the spurt of liquid. The *pro* disappears into the *jet*, it's Miller's whale spout . . . who was probably thinking of Melville's . . .

AVR: Rilke insists on the rhythm of writing. One can intend this for all the arts: the rhythm of a melody, but also the rhythm of a drawing, a painting. Is there one art that is more favorable than others to the experience of *jouissance*?

JLN: That's the question of the multiplicity of perceptible systems. Our relationship to the senses is originally multiple, and the diversity of senses cannot be arranged according to a hierarchy where there would be a superior sense, like sight or hearing. Philosophers have done much to classify the senses, with a metaphysical aim. But in art, our relationship to the senses is necessarily plural, because there is a diversity of forms and artistic practices, essential to the very idea of "form," but also because realms of the senses circulate through all the arts.

Artistic media are used a lot in their metaphorical sense: line, melody, color . . . Rilke insists on rhythm because it is present both in the arts and in sex. Think of the rhythm of the caress, for example. The come-and-go evoked in Gainsbourg's song: "*Je vais et je viens, entre tes reins, et je me retiens . . .*"[4] The caress cannot be motionless; it is by definition always in movement. Simple contact is not enough; there is always the expectation or the promise of a caress. The movement of the caress travels over the entirety of a body, pausing on certain zones, the ones we call erogenous. According to Freud, the entire body can be an erogenous zone, but we speak of "zone" to designate what is not a functional part, what is not organic. So the caress has a twofold movement: the path it takes, and the come-and-go. This come-and-go consists of repeating, that is, in Latin, of asking again for it. The zone is where you pass, linger, you "*zone*,"[5] you come back to it . . .

Rhythm in general is born from what is never definitively there, from what does not stay in place and causes us to return, what leads to *jouissance*. Rhythm is fundamental for humans, but for nature as well; think of the rhythm of the stars. And sex and the nighttime are often linked, probably for questions of invisibility: In Miller's text, it's because it's night that the narrator and Mara can make love on a sidewalk. At night, one enters into another space, less visible but denser, into another time, too. Time doesn't pass in the same way, which induces a special rhythm to the sexual act, even though we don't only make love at night.

AVR: The rhythm that leads to *jouissance* can also be thought of in a visual way, even in a colorful way. I'm thinking of the rhythms present in colors, for example.

JLN: Yes, there is a rhythm of colors present in painting. A painter's palette expresses his rhythmic relationship to colors. But color has a very special quality: It's a form that needs something other than itself in order to exist. To distinguish one color from another, you need rupture, which is drawing in the general sense, that is to say the line, whether it's intentional or not; otherwise all colors would exist only in the form of a blur or blend. I often imagine a painting in which all the colors begin to drip and would thus become indistinct. So color needs line in order to exist, but on the other hand, there is nothing visible without color. A colorless line is no longer a line, a colorless flower could not be seen. Color is an *expression* in the most literal sense: It's the pressure outward, a summons to the outside. Of course, this can be explained in chemical terms: A flower has such-or-such a color in order to attract insects and butterflies. But this explanation does not allow us to take into account the intensity of a certain red or a certain green, its density, which makes it the location of an extraordinary sensuality. The importance of texture can be understood if one tries for example to transfer the green of a tree leaf to a sheet of paper or a piece of cloth. On a different surface, the green changes its aspect, its gleam, its flesh.

It's in this sense that we can understand color as an exuberance, an orgasm [*jouissance*] of a thing. This is true, too, for soft colors. The first meaning of *chroma*, in Greek, is complexion, the color of the skin, and *color*, in Latin, designates something that covers in order to make distinct; it contrasts with *corpus*, "body." It's a distinction, a differentiation [*mise en valeur*].

AVR: Color is also seduction by body—eyeshadow, makeup.

JLN: It attracts and opens to possible pleasure [*jouissance*]. But it's because this seduction can in itself be a pleasure [*jouissance*] that it has been subject to condemnation. There's a whole complex history of color in religions . . .

THE CONDEMNATION
OF *JOUISSANCE*

ADÈLE VAN REETH: We have seen with Sade that *jouissance* could be born from pain inflicted on another or on oneself. So suffering can be at the origin of pleasure. From this origin a moral condemnation is born on the part of religion or society, which explains how *jouissance* has been forbidden and hence experienced guiltily. Christianity rests on a founding condemnation of pleasure, which is conceived of as an act of disobedience to God, as when Eve bit into the forbidden fruit and thus condemned humans to be sinners and guilty from birth. Here, the issue is no longer aesthetic but moral: On what basis can *jouissance* be condemned?

JEAN-LUC NANCY: Christianity marks a huge caesura in the history of humanity. Why did Christianity win? I've asked historians the question many times. Paul

Veyne, in his book *Quand notre monde est devenu chré-tien* [*When Our World Became Christian*], explains that unlike what we might be led to believe, the conversion of the Roman Empire to Christianity under Constantine was not a politically motivated maneuver because Christians didn't represent a real force at the time. In fact, Constantine was surrounded by intellectuals of great quality who saw in the discourse spoken by the Christians a calming answer to the profound anxiety and agitation that beset the population at the time. It was a very troubled period. I think of the phrase of a German historian that Freud quotes in *Moses and Monotheism* and which says in effect, "In the two centuries preceding Christianity, a great sadness seems to have taken hold of all the peoples of the Mediterranean." These centuries correspond to the rise of Stoicism, the dominant philosophy, but also of Epicureanism and Cynicism. These philosophies are in search of what Foucault has called concern for self, and which was like a rampart against the hostility of a world that had entered a state of perdition, wandering, and anguish. It was the end of the great theocratic regimes, and with them the disappearance of agrarian cults. How then to organize a world henceforth deprived of its familiar divine order? It's at that point that the now classic question of how to lead one's life arose. Conduct was no longer a given. One had to trace one's path in the midst of a world that had changed, which had become disorganized, both as a cosmic world and as a human world.

The latter had become the place of power and violence, but also of a wealth that Marx calls pre-Capitalist and that took the form of accumulation and profit, rather than ostentation or the sacred.

Simultaneously, this torsion of the world gave rise to an explosion of technological inventions, which went from writing to the use of iron, including navigational techniques, that were concomitant with the appearance of politics and philosophy. Now these would also experience a crisis, as shown by the Roman Empire itself. The Empire was already the sign that the Republic was doing poorly since it deified a man and made him an emperor. In this context, Christianity appears as one possible solution to the political problem: Whereas Rome deified a sovereign, Christianity, on the contrary, humanized God. Obviously, an entirely different relationship of man to the world followed. What Christianity brought that was new was a concept of human life as passage over Earth, with the idea that the essential lies elsewhere, in another world, that of the spirit.

I've lingered over this point of history a little, but I think it's important for our topic for us to have a good grasp of this division between two worlds, which was no accident but which evolved from within our history.

AVR: Life as passage, but also as suffering, as the Passion of Christ and even the Biblical text itself attest.

JLN: In the Passion of Christ lies the source of a *jouissance* made of redemptive suffering [*une jouissance* *doloriste*] that extends throughout the entire history of painting, as if there were an extraordinary ambivalence in this cruel execution that is willed by God and that is the actual sanctification of the man who calls himself the Son of God. God has emptied himself of His divinity, He has become mortal. This mortality is felt both as the death of God himself, as Luther would proclaim it much later on, but also as the divinization of the life of man. Human truth is henceforth divided in half: One must pass through suffering in order to reach salvation. So suffering is attached to the world here below and, in a sense, now the flesh can be nothing but guilty. Note that guilt is not a Christian invention: There was also a lot of sexual regulation in the Stoic and even Epicurean climate. It's fundamental in thinking of *jouissance* because, in a way, starting from that, all earthly pleasures become evil: sexual pleasure but also the pleasure of power.

Earthly pleasures become evil and even more powerful. For, in fact, sin is less a fault in the usual sense (a breach of law) than a rivalry between the two worlds (flesh and spirit), an intense rivalry. Heavenly joy and jubilation inaugurate a rivalry with human joy and *jouissance*. Perhaps there is in this an excess of pleasure [*jouir*] . . .

AVR: From *libido sentiendi,* sensual desire, to *libido dominandi,* which is the desire to dominate . . .

JLN: The latter is more decisive than we think. And for us, today, power has a negative connotation. We don't recognize anymore its own right to be power. But the present political scene shows more and more the urgency to revive a *libido dominandi*: Without this desire for power, there can be no politicians. Today this desire manifests in its naked, almost obscene state, as with Berlusconi. The taste for domination is probably also a component in *jouissance*, but it is more a question of being dominated by excess. The problem is that the general image of sexuality interprets power as being essentially masculine. And power is not necessarily omnipotence: It can also manifest in the form of a modulation of energy, a rhythmic game that by turns contains and frees it.

What we must keep in mind is that the condemnation of the flesh—concomitant with Christianity, which interprets *jouissance* as evil—is this consequence: the disappearance of a world ordered by divine, sacred presences, in which sexuality was very coded, but not condemned. In *Tristes Tropiques*, Lévi-Strauss describes the Nambikwara couples who, after the meal that gathers everyone together at the end of the day, leave to make love behind the bushes, for privacy rather than for concealment. It's in this context that Lévi-Strauss speaks of happy laughter, that is, laughter expressing desire experienced in a non-guilty way.

AVR: But though Christianity leads to a concept of sexuality that is necessarily evil and on the side of sin, that still does not mean it renounces all notion of *jouis-*

sance. Joy is very present in Christianity, even though it is always associated with a beyond, in the form of a mystical communion with God, notably.

JLN: Absolutely. Communion is a Christian word but one that has been widely used in the amorous and erotic register: Lovers commune in love. This word is an apple of discord between Bataille and Blanchot, in their ways of thinking about community. I myself wrote, at the time, that "communion" is a word that we seek to avoid but around which everything revolves. We want to avoid it because it is Christian, but also because it indicates something impossible: If communion is union in a single body, then that body becomes unique, and we wind up with the suppression of the "*co*," of that "with" that we need in thinking of two beings. But Christian communion consists of entering into what we call the mystical body of Christ, becoming a member of that body while still remaining a separate body, a subject. The mystical body of Christ recalls Hobbes's *Leviathan*: a great number in com-position, a body of body.

To take the measure of the influence of Christianity on our concept of *jouissance*, we must look at the situation in non-Christian cultures. Read Egyptian and Mesopotamian love poems, Chinese erotic texts... One thing is definite: Nowhere is sex conceived of as commonplace, like food; it always contains a sacred nature, in the sense of being separate, apart. Still this sacred nature seems less stamped with prohibitions and fears. I think of that big Chinese novel[1] whose central theme concerns a man who has pieces of a dog's penis grafted onto his own penis after noticing that when a dog has penetrated a bitch, its penis swells more and cannot be removed—so that when we see dogs coupling, we can't do anything to separate them. This character, by attaching a new property to himself, thinks he'll become more virile.

AVR: But if sexuality seems described more freely in the non-Christian texts you mention, can we still say that *jouissance* is more called into question in them? One does not imply the other . . .

JLN: This is the case in Japanese woodblock prints. Many of these prints represent *jouissance* by an exaggerated exhibition of the sexual organs, sometimes monstrously enlarged, and by particular positions. The act is presented completely, often with a character who is watching from behind a screen, which adds a voyeuristic dimension.

In Western Antiquity, it seems to me that despite the sacred status of sexuality, there is no prohibition specifically of having an orgasm. (One has only to remember Plato's *Phaedrus*.) Whereas Christianity makes this prohibition explicit by giving it a very singular allure: Authorized copulation is solely in order to produce children, with one exception for men who can mate simply in order to discharge (themselves) because Paul said it was better to marry oneself than to burn in place! No reference is made to the woman's pleasure. Much later, nightgowns were invented with holes at the pubic area so that they didn't have to be removed during the act . . . There was here a kind of fierce reversal of the rivalry I was speaking about: for the Christian, joy has become somber, evil . . . It has grown afraid of itself.

Aside from Christianity, *jouissance* is present and described as a jolt, not just in literature. In the *Phaedrus*, Plato describes the lover like a bird that puffs out its feathers, and ends up ejaculating . . . in one sense, it's very obscene! I always wonder how this text of Plato's came to be welcomed into the literature of the time. Because later, in the *Symposium*, *jouissance* has become higher, of a spiritual order. How do we explain this evolution? Perhaps Plato is here a witness of what will become the malaise of ancient civilization which hasn't managed to construct a divine order and thus has become a civic religion. As for Socrates, he breaks with civic religion by not respecting the gods of the city. Perhaps we can see in Plato the beginning of this movement that results in the invention of the idea of a spiritual *jouissance* distinct from physical *jouissance*. Pascal says that Plato was preparing the way for Christianity . . .

AVR: Note that as soon as physical *jouissance* is banned or condemned, it is immediately transferred to something else, whether it's God or power. As if this desire to *jouir* could not be removed from humans, so that it would be a necessity more than a desire . . .

JLN: Absolutely. And that's probably the case in all eras and in all societies.

AVR: But then how are we to understand this condemnation? You said that the desire for power was necessary for the smooth functioning of the body politic—hence there is a good use for the *jouissance* of power, concomitant with human civilization. So *jouissance* would be a component of man, but it's as if he could not accept himself as a *jouisseur*, as if he had to prevent himself from *jouir* even when he knew he was a *jouissant*! It's a problem that's both moral and anthropological.

JLN: You are right to say that this condemnation of *jouissance* is not just a moral one. But perhaps the prohibition is necessary for *jouissance*. In all the pages in Plato on sexual seduction and pleasure, on the pleasure of drinking wine in the *Symposium*, none condemns *jouissance*. But can we really speak of *jouissance*? There is indeed a jolt, an excitement, but they develop into beauty. The spasm is not entirely the *"petite mort"* [orgasm, "the little death"—Trans.] that is at issue for example in Hemingway, unless the *"petite,"* here, signifies precisely a making of *"mort"* into beauty [*mise en beauté*] . . .

For there to be morality, whence condemnation, there must be an idea of evil, and this evil must be presented as a danger. It's a vicious circle: There is danger because it's evil, and evil because there is danger. In a way, the aesthetic, and even spiritual, value must not come first; it is the pleasure of wine, the pleasure of the sight of beautiful bodies, which must pass from beautiful bodies to beautiful souls. This passage gives meaning and virtue to pleasure. What is reversed, with Christianity, is the entrance of these pleasures into morality, by way of their condemnation in the name of a danger: death without resurrection. But it's as if this very gesture truly freed the kernel of *jouissance*. The point of excess that is the characteristic of *jouissance* is both ecstatic and dangerous. If you detach the joyful, rejoicing dimension from *jouissance*, what remains is something that makes you tremble. A trembling, a jolt, by which the Platonic lover is himself seized. The reality of *jouissance* is that of a spasm that occurs once an extremity is attained, in the form of contraction and explosion. But to conclude, one cannot detach the disturbance of the trembling or ignore the threshold of propriety.

For Plato, it's the point from which one can go further. One can, like Socrates, drink and not get drunk . . . The others have collapsed, they're snoring on the table, while he is already outside and going about his business, though he has drunk as much as they. Who has had pleasure [*qui a joui*], in the story? Either the drink has no effect on him, in which case we don't understand why he would continue to drink, or it pleases him, and we have to understand that drinking makes him pass into another sort of drunkenness, a spiritual drunkenness that is not a failing [*déchéance*].

We come back to the idea of a failing, present in sin. The major change, from Plato to Christianity, is the subjectification of *jouissance*. In Christianity, *jouissance* happens to a subject, which is not the case in Plato. Of course, there is indeed someone who is seized by the force of *jouissance* and who experiences it, but it would be truer to say that he is between rejoicing and joy, and not in *jouissance*, which can only be expressed in the first person: I am coming [*je jouis*] . . . The Platonic lover does not say: I am coming. And Plato does not privilege virginity. Yet even after Christianity, Duchamp speaks of his "Bride" as one whom "*jouissance* will cause to fall [*déchoir*]" . . .

AVR: But does someone who sees himself as a sinner in *jouissance* say "I'm coming!"? He doesn't have the right!

JLN: Sade is a "good" Christian, and if the hero in Sade blasphemes, it's because he knows he's dealing with the forbidden. The Platonic lover, though, does not know that. Saint Augustine reflects on this simultaneity of awareness both of the prohibited and of the birth of the subject, which occurs along with the invention of intimacy. Remember the famous phrase of Augustine: "*Interior intimo meo superior summo meo*," "You are more inward than my own inwardness, higher than the highest summit of myself." This phrase occurs in an address to God, so it's an exclamation. The *Confessions* are entirely an address of the "I" to God: I confess, I talk to you; before I didn't know who you were, but now I know you. And when I know you I say: You are more inward, more intimate, than my own inwardness.

AVR: The *Confessions* signal the birth of the "I" in literature, as if, with Christianity, the condemnation of *jouissance* coincided with the birth of the subject, of the "I" who does not have the right to *jouir*.

JLN: When Augustine says "more inward than my own inwardness" and "higher than the summit of myself," one might think he is actually in *jouissance*, like that traversed subject we were discussing earlier. He lets himself be taken by God at the same time as he is enjoying [*jouit*] his own triumph over the powers of Evil, as he is enjoying his own conversion and what he accuses himself of at the beginning of the *Confessions*, namely, his skill as a rhetorician. The irony is that he accuses himself of a lot, but this remorse is for him the opportunity for a beautiful moment of rhetoric!

Rhetoric is a sin of vanity and an aesthetic sin, the sin of taking too much pleasure in handling speech. Among the other sins Augustine accuses himself of, the most important one is that of having loved love instead of loving God. It's a formulation that synthesizes Christian morality, but can't we understand in it a phrase of *jouissance*? "To love love" signifies that it's not a person one loves, but love itself, which comes down to saying that one loves making love ... or that love pleases itself in making love [*l'amour se plaît à se faire*].

The only person who deserves to be loved is God, and if one loves someone else, it should be in relation to God. Augustine says he loves his mother, who is a holy woman, but the prohibition of incest is present without there even being any need to mention it.

What does Augustine tell us? That *jouissance* is necessarily the *jouissance* of a subject, without the subject being the origin of it. It's the experience the subject can have of losing himself, of no longer being present to himself. That is why Augustine's phrase, *interior intimo meo*, designates *jouissance* by the two ways that are inwardness [*intimité*] and superiority. Actually, both are in the same place, since if you represent the inward as the inside of the body (think of the private parts), then that which is more inward than inwardness is necessarily the outside. That is Augustine's rhetorical prowess! That is why one shifts over to greatness, to elevation beyond the summits. This exuberance makes me think of Bataille, who compares Jesus to a mountain whose summit is exploding, like Vesuvius—he says "Jesuvius." In both cases, it's an orgasmic image. Don't forget that the character who haunts this story of *jouissance* is Dionysus, the person of the orgy, of the orgiasm, which gave us the term orgasm. At the height of the inward, at the summit, one topples over.

Moreover, the term *jouissance* is a noun that seems insufficient compared to the force of the verb *jouir* and to the exclamation "*je jouis!*," "I'm coming!" in which the subject becomes lost in the verb. The subject becomes wholly *jouissant*, as when the child says "I" for the first time: It's a form of jubilation.

What is true for *jouissance* is true for all great pain. This excess is felt in the same way by all *jouissants* and sufferers through the centuries. But the whole difference, which is very hard to represent to ourselves, is that it's not the same thing to say that it happens *to someone*, and to say merely that it happens. One must manage to think of *jouissance* and pain either as phenomena that concern a society as a whole: Either the social whole shares the emotion, channels it and symbolizes it, or else, on the contrary, it refers to each person, it nestles in the inwardness of each person. As if, at a given moment, humanity said: But that's happening to me, to *me*!

FROM PROFIT TO CONSUMPTION/ CONSUMMATION

Can We Enjoy Everything?

ADÈLE VAN REETH: You mention the place of the "I" inside a larger whole in which it is inscribed and which vastly surpasses it. This is an experience we can have in the West with the distance that separates the subject from the collective. But the collective recovery of *jouissance* can transform it into a slogan, a demand, which seems completely detached from the experience of *jouissance*. I'm thinking of the phrase "*jouissez sans entraves*" [enjoy without restrictions] that was written on the walls in '68, for example. The collective dimension in question here is very different from the one you've just discussed in connection with Christianity.

JEAN-LUC NANCY: No, that's true! The idea of collectivity, or community, appeared with Judaism, when

Antiquity had lost it: Plato wasn't much interested in it, Aristotle a little more so, but the collective was reduced to politics, thus to questions of organization of the city. Whereas Christianity was founded right away on a community. May '68 was part of a much longer time. The explosion was social at its root, but also came from a discrepancy between the condition of university teaching and the actual state of economic and technological development of society at that time. To that was added—and this I think was especially important—a weariness with the great Communist project. Communism is a word that comes from Christianity. From the end of the eighteenth century, the term began to express a certain demand, a requirement born from the collapse of Christianity as an organization of the whole society: Christendom was a community, which appears very clearly in the feudal form. But monarchy and the appearance of the modern State would divide individuals in a different way, until the invention of capitalism, which would insert the individual subject into the circuit of a new *jouissance*: no longer the *jouissance* of excess, but that of accumulation and investment. It's a *jouissance* that can no longer bear that name.

AVR: Why? What has changed?

JLN: It's simple: When wealth is hoarded, it accumulates in hands supposed to be the worthiest and is transformed into glorious, spiritual power. Look at the Strasbourg Cathedral: Imagine the number of people, the stones they had carried over the Rhine, the labor, the money required . . . Of course that represented an investment for the Church, but they couldn't calculate the amortization!

There is an important rupture between this form of wealth and that of accumulation of capital ready for investment which was made possible by the invention of the bank and of paper money. The birth of capitalism was the Lombard bankers swarming all over Europe. More than an economy, it was a new way of life, a new society in which production was dominant: You had to produce in order to consume, and produce more to consume even more. That is the rise of something that had always existed as a luxury (but royal glory is not bourgeois luxury . . . and the king's pleasure [*jouissance*] is not that of a President of the Republic) and which now became a kind of social norm of behavior, of desirability. In his *Critique of Pure Reason*, Kant notes that the people of his time were working more and more to produce more luxury, and he laments that so many people are using their strength and their lives to produce what only a small number of people will enjoy.

AVR: But don't we have to distinguish *jouissance* from profit? The two can be opposites.

JLN: That's true, but the problem is that *jouissance* today is partly confused with profit. In this new society, *jouissance* is on one hand linked to profit, on the other to property. Which is at bottom the opposite of *jouis-*

sance understood as excess, since property offers the possibility of bringing excess back to itself—of "locking it up," if I can put it that way. The excessive changes its meaning: From exuberant it becomes appropriating. We could speak of a subjectification of excess, which at the same time annuls excess and subject, enjoyment and the "one" who enjoys [*le jouir et le "qui" jouit*].

AVR: In the sense that one can enjoy being a property owner?

JLN: In the sense that property is no longer opposed to excess because it *becomes* excess, and because of this, loses its meaning. It's the good infinite that becomes the evil infinite. Excess takes on a numerical meaning: It's a question of possessing the greatest possible quantity. In the history of *jouissance*, this is fundamental: At this time, our time, *jouissance* is understood in its first meaning, that is, its legal, not sexual, meaning. It has left heaven, joy, to land again on earth.

It's important to understand the summons to enjoy without restrictions of May '68: The word *jouissance* was not understood then as it is today, as a kind of jubilation or sexual frenzy. It was applied to a consumption of objects and bore the mark of words and thoughts that were very important in the history of Christianity: covetousness, greed, concupiscence . . . all these words that truly designate the heart of evil. *Jouissance* was "restricted" by definition. '68 wanted to free itself of bourgeois, petty sin, not to consume outrageously.

So we have to keep in mind that in '68, the proper legal sense of *jouissance* was reserved for the lawyers, and reference to greedy consumption did not yet arise. Thus, the call to enjoy without restrictions simply meant that it was society that prevented people from enjoying. Society was perceived as subjecting individuals to a machine of production and consumption that people were realizing led nowhere. In other words, it was appearing clearly that Communism had failed, or had never really happened. Communism, for Marx and for many after him, was thought of as an immense *jouissance* for everyone because the goods produced could return to those who were producing them. A *jouissance*, then, that was understood as a consumption. My second-year German teacher at the Ecole Lakanal, Pierre Juquin, was a member of the Communist Party and had written a poem that ended with "more of everything for everyone," like a great hymn to Communism—already seven or eight years before '68. This poem was like a kind of breathless last scrap of something in which no one believed anymore and which was moreover extraordinarily ambiguous . . . Enjoy or consume? Spasm or repletion?

AVR: Since Communism was thought of as a kind of *jouissance* of all by all that had failed, then May '68, by calling on people to enjoy [*jouir*] without restrictions, was offering a new way to enjoy, including by heralding a summons for sexual liberation. Which marks a break from a generation that couldn't manage to *jouir*.

JLN: Absolutely. It resembles the project in the very beginning of the Communist revolution in Russia. Next to the aesthetic avant-garde—of painters, poets, musicians—there were also people who were advocating free love, which was far from what Lenin had in mind! In Western Europe there had already been a few upheavals, some aesthetic and moral jolts, a disturbance of aesthetic practices and customs, which occurred between Baudelaire and Rimbaud. It was the beginning of a society of production and consumption. "Enjoy without restrictions," then, meant: Liberate the possibility of enjoying, represented mainly at that time by sex, which they wanted to detach completely from family and social restraints—but not yet other forms of *jouissance*. A huge ambiguity, once again, was at work: that of sex and drugs.

At that time there began something that considerably increased the modes of addiction in our society. Today, addiction has become a psychoanalytic and psychiatric specialty. The word comes from England, but in the Latin sense [*adictum*] it designates a preference, a penchant. Starting in the nineteenth century with opium addicts, it took on the modern sense of enslavement. So the word went from penchant or tendency to dependence. From tendency to dependency: It sounds like a slogan! And everything is at stake here. The young adults in '68, of whom I was one, had absolutely no mistrust of dependency. Whereas today, if there is one question to ask ourselves, it's that of finding out why our society is an addictive society, more so than ever before, I think. Addiction is a reversed, destructive *jouissance.*

AVR: Don't you think that this passage from tendency to dependency is also the result of moral, or even governmental, condemnation? In the sense that the more the consumer of harmful substances is vilified, the more he's made into an incurable addict. Today, "enjoy without restrictions" would not make sense because the enjoyment [*jouissance*] of someone who harms himself by pleasing himself—like the smoker—is perceived as destructive by all of society. Hasn't the moralizing and medical public discourse directed at dependency eclipsed *jouissance*?

JLN: Yes, that's a good question, which is part of those insoluble problems that prove Marx wrong when he said, "Man poses only those problems for himself that he can solve." Unless he's right over the long term . . . Because these problems of public health arose at the same time as the State and as a whole ensemble of mechanisms taking charge of public health. But what Foucault called biopolitics is simply the fact that politics, or rather administrative procedures, became extremely complex and had to interfere in all fields because now there is only one world, a single reticular, tentacular complex.

Cars, for instance, became a nest of problems: People wonder what kind of fuel they use, if they're very polluting, if it would be better for them to be electric, how fast they're allowed to go on the highway, how many people can ride in them, if the seatbelts are securely attached ... I remember the beginning of obligatory seatbelt-wearing. I didn't have one when I had a very bad accident and I broke a hip; if my seatbelt had been attached, that would not have happened. But at the time many people protested against the seatbelt; it prevented you from freely enjoying driving ... And I remember very clearly noticing the moment when, in movies, we began systematically seeing people getting into a car and fastening their seatbelts.

AVR: How do you explain that? Is obsession with health and safety the new enemy of *jouissance*?

JLN: In any case, these obsessions affect the evolution of the concept we have of *jouissance*. But perhaps the enemy of *jouissance* is also in the desire to profit from an ever-increasing number of things. That's the case with the car, which we've always wanted to be as big and fast as possible. The car was born from the desire to move more quickly than on horseback and in a less tiring way. Before the car came the train, which introduced the collective dimension into transportation. The idea was to move more quickly and to go further with more people.

AVR: That said, one can enjoy speed. Wanting to go further and faster isn't necessarily opposed to *jouissance*.

JLN: Yes, but enjoying speed implies having the possibility of speed. Françoise Sagan describes well the pleasure of pressing down on the accelerator, your hand hovering over the stickshift . . . But the means had to be there. What interests me is trying to find out why we wanted access to more speed. First there was an economic imperative: The acceleration of means of transportation was connected to the circulation of merchandise. Here we find the fundamental motivation for capitalism, which is to make it so that wealth always produces more wealth, thus developing a general action of production that aims to produce even more. But we lack a third term, that of consumption: For this production to produce wealth, it must be consumed. For it to be consumed it must satisfy an expectation. For that expectation to exist . . . it must be created, we'd say today.

AVR: Capitalism as a need-creating machine?

JLN: And these needs were created by the same system that aims to respond to them. Once you've entered the system of production, there are no good reasons not to desire everything that's presented to you as accessible. In the past, the desire to have more, to go faster, could be aroused by the wish to navigate as far as possible: It was a question of having ships that were as big and solid as possible to transport merchandise and carry out exploration. The discovery of America was possible thanks to this process, which is much older than we imagine. The royal *ateliers* in France of Louis

XIV were already factories. A factory is a large gathering of workers and buildings aiming to produce, for example, immense ropes for rigging ships. The logic of modern society was already there: to create a unit of labor and production. Then came the steam engine, born from scientific curiosity, which at once created new needs, because it allowed ships to go much faster. This process was accompanied, until the end of the nineteenth century, by the possibility that society could give itself new images that created a new aesthetic world. Turner painted steamships and took great pleasure in mixing golden glints with the smoke coming from the ships. But little by little, the modern world seems to have found it difficult to take pleasure from itself [*jouir de lui-même*] . . .

AVR: Do you think that the idea of *jouissance* has lost its meaning today?

JLN: I think it has meaning only for those who are on the right side of profit. Those who pile up profit in the most active and enterprising spirit of capitalism, who aren't content to accumulate but who are also in venture, risk, calculation of profitability. Some are real geniuses at this, like Bill Gates. But the handling of financial technologies has developed at the same time as a middle-class has appeared, which made the great class struggle unthinkable. Instead, we have witnessed the overflowing of a middle-class made up of those who had to be content with limited savings, and others who, less small, could invest their savings in stocks. It's the beginning of what we call the market, which is now controlled by large financial and economic groups.

AVR: It gives rise to a new *jouissance*: that of risk-taking, challenges, speed . . .

JLN: Of course! That's the case for those who are exactly at the forefront of both accumulation and risk. I'm sure that at Google, there are teams who must be very proud of and happy with what they do. It's also the case for video games, which represent a major market today. When I discovered my first video game, my youngest son was quite young and I hurried to get him in front of the computer to show him how he could play with it. Today, I wonder if I'm responsible for his relationship to video games, which seems to have become a dependency. For video games can be, for some, a kind of social disease. But that's not a general law, once again: to play and to enjoy [*jouer et jouir*], the two words have nothing in common—but one shouldn't go without the other. But profit-making *jouissance* isn't play: It dwells in the anguish of satisfaction, it lies in addiction.

AVR: But is the video-game industry really responsible? Before they came on the scene, lots of other ways to enclose yourself in a virtual world existed. Perhaps what you seem to be deplore might not be attributed to one particular development in society, but rather reveals a constant of humanity: the need to play, but also the necessity, sometimes, to turn one's back on reality, or to create another reality for oneself.

JLN: That's true, but perhaps it's easier today to enclose yourself in another universe. It seems to me that, since May '68, many young people don't much want to enter into this society, and seek instead to flee it.

AVR: Because society is no longer perceived as the place for possible *jouissance*? Or else is it a question of a loss of interest in *jouissance* in general, which would go against a discourse that deplores the loss of interest in anything that isn't *jouissance*?

JLN: Most analysts say that we're in a society of *jouissance* that they describe as narcissistic. I have to admit that addiction seems to me the sign that our relationship to *jouissance* has become more destructive. Tobacco, alcohol, video games, and the games of financial traders lead to a totality of behaviors in which the creative *jouissance* of an elsewhere is absent. Twenty or thirty years ago, you could have the feeling you were advancing things by doing philosophy or music. In the 1970s and into the early '80s, society was carried along by the idea that it was making progress. We even thought we were progressing in relation to the idea of progress! People had the conviction that what they were doing could transform life, or at least society. "Change your life" was also a motto from '68, and the desire for change was clearly going toward more *jouissance*, but "more" in the sense of finer, keener, more exalting.

That said, I'm extremely mistrustful of analysts who hurry to say that the fact of watching television is always a sign of isolation. And the last time I praised the virtues of the Smartphone in an interview, they thought I was crazy! It's true that there is a malaise in civilization but it's not excess, it's a lack of *jouissance*.

AVR: That has often been the case in the past.

JLN: Except today, we no longer know where to turn. Today what could assume the roles that in the past were played by religion, politics, technical innovation? We lack motivation [*élan*]. Including in the realm of aesthetics.

AVR: Is that so definite? Look at the dynamic quality of cinema in France and throughout the world. We've never produced so much. Cartoons and graphic novels are also doing well. For contemporary art, music, literature, it's more complicated because we usually need a generation to pass before we consider an author as a genius.

JLN: You put your finger on the problem: the difficulty we have in thinking about the present in terms of the possibility of a future that is positive. In the 1950s and '60s, there was a word that no longer exists today: prospect, *prospective*. It was even the name of a journal. I'm thinking of Bertrand de Jouvenel, of Teilhard de

Chardin . . . In their way of thinking we found a form of naivety close to that of old-fashioned communist progressives . . . What I'm calling naivety was a way of still believing in an ideal. Since then, though, we are convinced there is no political ideal, or any ideal at all. That's true if the "ideal" is idealistic, but *jouissance* is not. It is . . . enthusiastic, overwhelmed . . .

I agree with you about the facile quality of a defeatist discourse about the present and contemporary aesthetic production. Even in video games, there is certainly a resourcefulness, an inventiveness that I never suspected. And that's especially true for the cinema that, in twenty years, has put us in another relationship with the world by no longer offering—or offering less of—dreams and fables, but an engagement with the real that is fascinating.

How can the term *jouissance* become "disreputable"? Perhaps because *jouissance* has become a synonym for what is designated as narcissism, self-satisfaction.

AVR: Perhaps, too, it's hard for us to think of *jouissance* in terms of the present, of immediacy, spontaneity, and because it's often easier to condemn the contemporary than to praise it.

JLN: It is very hard for us to think of the present, what is happening in the instant. Yet *jouissance*, precisely, requires an attention to the instant; it is in a presence that conceals itself as a present thing, but remains as an opening. Many philosophers wonder how to think of the present: Kierkegaard and Nietzsche tried to give it value. Kierkegaard thought of the instant in relation to the absolute; Nietzsche could only think of it with "the eternal return" and "I love you O eternity." These two ways of thinking are like a reaction against the great historic vision of accomplishment; they are incentives to which we always return. Foucault, Deleuze, Derrida, Lacan have also tried to think of the present, with the same difficulties, and also with their own findings and ways of *jouir* . . .

We'd have to manage to grasp a thought of the present through actions, modalities of action, what shapes a society. I wonder if we've managed to grasp the thought that presided over capitalism, and which led to this transformation of civilization worldwide. Why, at a particular moment, did Western society veer toward a way of thinking that advocated the general equivalence of merchandise? If we had this knowledge, we'd be better able to face the present, without having the impression of being stuck in a machine that keeps spinning . . . But that's an illusion of control. We have to know how to enjoy letting go of control: Thinking about the present demands it. Attention to the present must be a tension without anxiety, a desire without greed . . .

AVR: Isn't it also a question of character? Camus wrote, in *Summer in Algiers*: "It requires a rare vocation to be a sensualist [*jouisseur*]."[1] What's more we often underestimate, in philosophy, the question of character and temperament. From the absurdity of human existence a comedy (Woody Allen) or a tragedy (Kafka) can be born.

JLN: I'm the first to think that we underestimate this question. For a very long time I was of an optimistic disposition that was imperturbable, and sometimes criticized, but after coming up against scandalous realities, I can no longer say that today. Think of what is the opposite of *jouissance*, or of what in any case goes in a radically opposite direction: the increase of poverty in the developed countries, not to mention all the others. Or the multiplication of wars in the world. Of course, the gap between the poor and the rich has always existed, but before, the poor kept their heads to the ground, they didn't move, they said to themselves it was normal for the lord to own more than they did. Whereas today, everyone is scandalized to see that the head of a company can own so much. So we invent laws, we perform political antics around these questions, but none that's really effective to prevent managers from continuing to earn more and more and others less and less.

Have you noticed how much society loves to denounce itself? I see in this the sign of a slightly perverse *jouissance*. You just have to open any magazine, listen to or watch any "social issues" telecast: They attack platitudes and stigmatize as absolute evil the presence of tourists in shorts talking on their cell phones in front of Notre Dame Cathedral . . . On this point, I think that we philosophers are in charge of shedding light on what is happening. We can't be content to say, "You're wrong, enjoy the instant and all will be well!" To illumine something, you need light. To turn the light on you need not so much an energy source as the art of a "*fiat lux!*" And this art is connected to the "character" you speak of: Every time it's a tone, a way, even an idiom . . . There is no single light.

AVR: Yet not many philosophers speak directly of *jouissance*.

JLN: Yes, that's quite surprising. I could cite a few: Heidegger, at the end of his *Interpretation of Anaximander*, discusses his philosophy of the "presence of the present," which is endowed with a value of *jouissance*, or at least *réjouissance* [rejoicing], which is quite rare with him. Hegel ends his entire system by talking about "the eternal Idea that is in and for itself, makes itself active, creates itself, and eternally enjoys itself [*jouit de soi*] as absolute Spirit."[2] And Derrida said, "Whenever there is '*jouissance*' [. . .] there is 'deconstruction.'"

The inquiry among philosophers is surely not over yet. (To be complete, we'd have to speak of Levinas, Marion, and a few others: but the "property" [*propre*, distinctive feature]—if we can word it that way—of *jouissance* remains pending [*en souffrance*].) But it's still true that philosophy finds itself as if halted in front of *jouissance*—for two very different reasons. The first is the difficulty of thinking of completion, plenitude, without laying oneself open to a ponderousness and a forgetting of the infinite (with which Sartre, Levinas, Deleuze, and Lacan all have one—just one!—point in common). The second is the inability to create a concept to name that which bursts forth and goes elsewhere—outside of consciousness, self, the body itself, and the world. This "elsewhere" is not situated in the beyond: It is indeed here, but it escapes, flows away, disappears. But it is precisely this elsewhere that *jouissance* opens up—and closes on itself. It's a matter of thinking outside of concept . . .

One variation of this restraint [*retenue*] might be a kind of resistance to this escaping due to fear of suffering. Read Kant, paragraph 61 of his *Anthropology*: "To feel one's life, to enjoy oneself, is thus nothing more than to feel oneself continuously driven to leave the present state (which must therefore be a pain that recurs just as often as the present)."[3]

You quoted Camus praising the sensualist [*jouisseur*]. One might be tempted to say that "the sensualist" often designates rather one who accumulates, who is greedy, whereas Camus is thinking of one who is capable of pleasure, *jouissance*.

Limit or resistance? *Jouir* doesn't easily give itself to thought, or speech—or even experience: *Jouir* is inestimable; it is a way of feeling one's life.

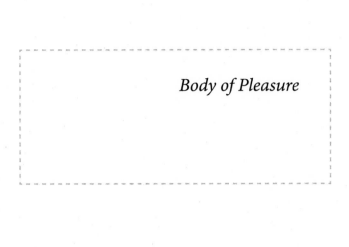

Body of Pleasure

1

What is a body of pleasure? It is a body freed from its perceptive and operative agendas. It no longer gives itself over to seeing or feeling in general according to the usual modalities of its functional, active, relational life. The body itself is no longer turned to the world, not even to the other with whom it exchanges (when it is a matter of sexual pleasure). There is no longer an "other" in the ordinary sense, although there is no sameness or fusion either. The two (or more, perhaps) beings are caught in a mingling that is not only a mingling of these different bodies, but at the same time a mingling in each one of its distinctions, roles or operations connected to the functions, actions, representations of everyday life—or rather, everyday or non-everyday life (for example the life of exertion in sport, an actor's performance, intense physical labor . . .) but rather commanded by—or subordinated to—some external outcome.

On the contrary, the body of pleasure is commanded only by itself. The body of pain acts similarly, but in the mode of refusing itself and rejecting itself, whereas pleasure keeps summoning itself and asking again and again for itself. What the former refuses and the latter demands is the same thing: a body re-composed (or de-composed, or over-composed) according to a composition different from one where its actions can engage it. It is a body mingled with itself and commanded by this mingling. Mingled with itself and with an other (or with others), with itself *as* with the other: becoming foreign to itself in order to relate to itself as to an other, or else to itself as the other approaches and trusts in it both to enjoy it (*jouir de lui*) and to rejoice itself (*réjouir lui-même*).

So the body of pleasure is not for itself except exactly insofar as it unburdens itself in itself of an 'auto-finality' on the order of self-preservation, maintaining its vital functions and technical abilities. What is conserved here, if we care to use that term (like Spinoza), or what is affirmed, is the body as ability to transform itself, re-form itself or, if you like, in-form (or else *ex-form*) itself—going from a conformation, or a conformity, regulated by a totality of social, cultural, technical practices, towards a form tendentially itself in constant formation.

This body invents, re-composes, re-plays itself. It re-forms itself and, if necessary, it ex-forms itself or de-forms itself so that it is nothing but an exposition of self: body as touching and touched skin, that is, modulation of an approach always begun again of its own limit as body. It touches its limit, reaches its limit, unlimits itself (*s'illimite*).

Tendentially, the body of pleasure is as unlimited as if it were no longer a body but rather pure soul. Just as the opposite movement of pain tends to reduce the suffering body to a suffering soul that is concentrated in burning and in its rejection of itself, or more exactly in that burning as it rejects itself. Pleasure and pain are, in fact, like two modes of being burned: a burning that feeds on itself or a burning that thrusts itself away from itself.

These are two modes in excitement: Excitement is the movement of solicitation by and response to an external agent. Excitability is a basic property of living beings. A living being is first of all excited: summoned to respond to an outside. Consequently, always already in response to this summons, always already excited, affected by an outside. Actually, it is this being-affected-by-an-outside that begins to make us live—whether as a plant or as a human animal.

(Because of this, it is understandable that the world has been represented as a great animal: the world is the living being excited by the empty outside, a non-world that it calls *nothing* or *god*, two equivalent terms to speak of this first touch.)

In pleasure and in pain, excitation is taken for itself, that is, even though the outside is at least comparable to this *nothing-god* of outside the world. It is not, in fact, the outside of the rest of the world to which excitation answers or reacts (*envoie, renvoie*) when it is a matter of perceiving, receiving and communicating, acting, and so on. But the outside is the body itself or nothing or another body as the *again* (*encore*) of an indefinite contact with the totality of bodies—of the world—contact through which tendentially it is to the extremity of the world, whether its creation or its end, that there is relation (*renvoi*).

To think about this, it is indispensable to liberate pleasure and pain from their goal-directed interpretations: pleasure (*plaisir*), here, is not the pleasurable (*agrément*) that indicates a useful or beneficial thing, and pain is not a signal warning of some harm. It's here we have to activate unreservedly the certainty of pleasure as *demand*: summons, incitation, excitation to go beyond usefulness and satisfaction in order to go towards the uncoupling of self, abandon, journey to the limit—a journey that does not cross that limit but that brushes up against it, touches and by touching lets itself be touched by the outside (nothing-god).

Any way of speaking of *jouissance* in terms of legal acceptance of full possession and hence repletion and satisfaction, of an "enough" with which a "self" is "content," remains prisoner of a confusion between *jouissance* (or joy) and that contentment we've just described. Being in contentment is also "to content oneself with." It's a measure of the useful and the reasonable. But pleasure is not content. That is even why it encloses a discontent where *jouissance* undoes itself under the excess of its own excitement. But these confines are precisely in the realms where the play of limits is played out, in closeness to pleasure and pain: impassable but touched, as touched crossed, but as touch pushing beyond that which could not go outside because this outside does not exist (is not another inside).

That the outside does not exist, and hence that it is outside—it places me outside of myself—is the experience of pleasure. In this sense, one can say that pleasure is always the infinite approach of pleasure—but that should not be understood in terms of disappointment or privation. No doubt it is legitimate to speak of "finitude" and to say that pleasure is finite: It is essentially, since it touches the end, that limit where the body tendentially loses all form and becomes matter, impenetrable mass. But this *end* also forms the touch of the outside and with it the joy of the world.

2

The body mingled with itself and another (or others), with itself *as* with the other, does not enter into an identification or into a confusion, but into a disturbing proximity because it *is* proximity, the approach of an uncertain differentiation and renewing, repetition and reviving a distancing where pleasure consists of tasting the measure forever uncertain, labile and trembling. To touch: that is, to make attraction and repulsion play together, wholeness and fracture, distinction and translation. Making the *totality* play as such, that is, brushing against unity and its release (*déprise*), its dis-union.

The body touched and touching—touched because it touches, touching because it is touched, always having elsewhere the sufficient reason of its being as body—this body commands itself, that is, this contact of bodies with no other aim than itself. Contact as well as with the same body as itself: for precisely it no longer is or has any more "self" but exposes itself wholly. It exposes itself first by placing itself outside the array of needs, functions, services, and purposes. Its purpose becomes the service of pleasure, which means: of movement by which a body recalls itself, gathers itself, and re-launches itself for itself, for its own resonance with the outside of bodies.

This body emerges from its form. Its heart no longer beats to the rhythm of a blood pump, but to that of an overwhelmed wildness; its lungs no longer breathe but pant, or even suffocate, in the attempt to breathe in a breath that would be the suspense of breath itself being traversed by wind. Its limbs are not limbs but de-form and re-form themselves into zones, parcels, or disoriented continents whose entire geography hollows out or swells according to the excitations that raise at each point the possibility of a complete re-composition. A body that departs wholly from a breast, a palm, a belly.

Among these zones are distinguished and exacerbated those that give rise to an effusion, a spurt or a stream of fluid, a solution, that is a dissolution of form in which an incessantly new possibility of form is outlined.

Everything is there, in the outline of an indeterminate re-composition whence another body emerges, another division of body, another mingling and unmingling of skins, a *liquidation*, in sum, of contours and organic and social constructions.

In sex, bodies bear witness to a calling to make themselves infinite beyond any tributary determination of any given order. That is why sex is the site of creation: making children or forming forms, assemblages and configurations, rhythms and resonances. Starting from nothing, that is, by opening widely what already of itself is nothing but opening: mouth, eye, ear, nostril, sex, anus, and skin, skin indefinitely taken up and re-opened by all its pores. Spreading open, largesse, catching up and letting go, going and coming, thrashing: always the syncopated cadence of a pace that carries us toward the confines of what a body first of all delimits.

The body of pleasure (and the body of pain as its opposite) un-limits the body. The same is true for transcendence.

Rühren, Berühren, Aufruhr
(Moving, Touching, Uprising)

Rühren, Berühren, Aufruhr: German lets us group in the same semantic family with *rühr* three notions to which we can match the French *bouger* or *agiter*; *toucher*; and *soulèvement*, or in English, *move* or *agitate*; *touch*; and *turmoil* or *uprising*, each of these terms understood according to the diversity of its shades of meaning. *Move* and *agitate* can be taken in both physical and moral senses, as well as *touch* and *uprising* (*toucher, soulève-ment*). The last term, for its part, orients its sense in a socio-political direction.

This semantic family involves movement, which is neither spatial movement (displacement, *Bewegung* in German) nor the movement of transformation (*Verwandlung* in German, metamorphosis, for example generation and corruption, growth and decline) but also movement that we could also designate as "emotion," a term that modalizes *motion*, the closest transcription of the Latin *motus*, from the verb *movere*, from which we have also preserved *move* and *be moved* (*mouvoir*, *émouvoir*).

Touch, in both French (*toucher*) and English, seems more foreign to the semantics of movement, whereas in German it clearly belongs to it. *Touch*, *tact*, or *contact* (*toucher*, *tact*, *contact*) seem more static than dynamic. Of course, we realize one must move in order to touch, one must "come into contact" as they say, but touching itself seems to me to designate a state rather than a movement, and contact suggests firm adhesion rather than a shifting process.

But both French and English are also very familiar with the mobile, driving, dynamic value of touching: this is present when we speak of a person or a work that "touches us," when we evoke the "touch" of a pianist or else the touch of a painter, and also the touch of divine grace.

Touching stirs us and makes us move. As soon as my body approaches another body—even if the latter is inert, made of wood, stone, or metal—I move (*déplace*) the other—even if only infinitesimally—and the other moves me away from it, holds me back in a way. Touching acts and reacts at the same time. Touching attracts and rejects. Touching pushes and draws back, impulse and repulsion, rhythm of the outside and inside, ingestion and rejection, proper and improper.

Touching begins when two bodies move away and make themselves distinct from each other. The child emerges from the womb and in turn becomes a belly that can swallow and spit out. It takes its mother's breast or its own finger in its mouth. Sucking is the first touch. Suction, of course, inhales nourishing milk. But it does something more, and something other: It closes its mouth over the body of the other. It establishes or re-establishes a contact by which it reverses the roles: the child who was contained now in turn contains the body that used to contain it. But it does not enclose it in itself; on the contrary: It holds it at the same time in front of itself. The movement of the sucking lips keeps repeating the alternation of closeness and distance, penetration and emergence, which presided over everything from the descent in the womb to the emergence out of the body of this new body finally ready to separate itself.

By separating itself, it conquers this new possibility it had known only sketchily before: the possibility of relationship (*rapport*) and contact. That sketchy outline was essentially auditory, and hearing itself was diffracted through the whole prism of the little body immersed in the resounding fluid with which the other body enveloped it. The sounds of that body—its heart, its intestines—and the sounds of the world outside touched its ears at the same time, touched its closed eyes, its nostrils, its lips, and all its submerged skin. "Touched," though, would be an overstatement. Every possible sensation was still diluted in an indistinct sense, in a constant, almost permeable exchange between outside and inside, as well as between the various openings in the body. "Touched" would be an overstatement and yet it's already there: It's the first *rühren*, the first wave and floating (*flot, flottement*) upon which what has not yet come to be born rocks.

When it is born, it will separate itself. But it will remain like that, female or male floating inside an element, within a world in which everything is related to everything, everything strives toward everything and moves away from everything—but this time following the multiple scansions of all the insides/outsides of separate bodies.

Only a separate body can touch. Only it can also separate entirely its touch from its other senses, that is, constitute in a single autonomous sense that which traverses all the senses, differentiating itself in them while still distinguishing itself as a kind of common reason. Reason or passion, impulse, motion.

Where there had been immersion, floating and enveloping from all sides in the relative non-differentiation of its outside and its inside, tendentially confused in the shared balancing of two bodies—where it had been sucking its own finger, now it detaches and, having come outside, finds itself facing this outside. That is, it is no longer inside the inside, no longer in immanence. In the truest sense of the word, it transcends: it passes beyond being in itself.

Its mobility leaves behind its suspended existence, its almost nonexistent weight, and the viscous indifference of directions. It becomes true movement depending on the distancing of other bodies. Far from seeking a return into immanence and immersion, its gestures affirm on the contrary its distinction, a separation that is not a privation or an amputation of anything. It is opening and relating. Relationship does not seek to restore indistinctness: it celebrates distinctness, it announces the encounter, that is, contact.

Actually, contact begins when the child begins to occupy almost all the space in which it has been floating. It comes to touch the walls and its movement becomes one of slow reversal that makes it capable of emerging, of letting itself be pushed from inside and breathe in from the outside—this time to espouse decisively the order of an inside/outside. Touching the limits of the vessel and the womb, it becomes like another wall and also like a wave ready to break and flow between the lips that will spread for it. This sliding is the ultimate form of a passage from floating to friction, from immanence to transcendence, and by opening the vulva it also opens all the distances that its separation will give rise to and through which real contact will become possible, at once distance and closeness, intimate extimacy.

Contact does not cancel separation; on the contrary. All the logics, metaphysical or psychological, that posit the primordial attraction of a supposed lost unity and the necessity to resign ourselves to this enforced separation—of severing, sexuation, of the plurality of senses, allures, aspects—are logics of a sort of monotheism or morbid monodeism. They are pathological—but they are not logics of *pathos* or of the *dunamis tou pathein* that is the ability to receive, the capacity to be affected. For affection is above all passion and movement of passion, of a passion whose very nature is "touching": to be touched, to touch in turn, to touch oneself with the touch that comes from outside, with the touch that touches me and with the touch by which I touch.

To be affected does not mean that a given subject comes, in a given circumstance, to receive an affection. How could one accept without being capable of doing so? But this capacity itself must be capacity in the truest sense of the word: ability to receive. To be able to receive already implies receiving, being affect-able. To be affected demands having been so, demands always already having been so. That is why there has always already been an outside and always already an opening up to the outside. Always already an opening straining toward the outside. A desire for the outside such as can only have been preceded by the outside, without which it could not be desired. The subject is not anterior or exterior to the outside, he is—if at least one wants to speak of subject—rather, as we can say in French, *sujet au dehors*, "subject to the outside": subject to the other, subject to the touch of the other. What begins as floating-becoming-friction in this vessel that is the amnion where the homunculus swims, it is just this touch of the outside.

When this vessel lets its contents pour out, water streams out and the child emerges from it, streaming. Its entire body—for the first time whole and detached—bears the moist imprint that becomes its skin, that melts into the outline of its skin but that makes this skin always capable of receiving the outside, of being bathed and swayed, rocked in the swells of the outside.

So touch first of all and always is this rocking, this floating and friction repeated by suction, renewing and re-playing the desire of feeling oneself touched and touching, the desire to experience oneself being in contact with the outside. More even than "in contact with" but contact itself. My entire being is contact. My entire being is touched/touching. Which is also to say open to the outside, opened through all my orifices—ears, eyes, mouth, nostrils—and of course all those channels of ingestion and digestion like those of my liquids, sweats, and sexual fluids. As for the skin, it sets about spreading out around these openings, these entrances-and-exits, becomes an envelope that just as it situates them and specifies them, it develops for itself this capacity to be affected and to desire it. Each sense specializes affect appropriate to a distinct domain—seeing, hearing, smelling, tasting—but the skin constantly connects these different domains to one another without confusing them. The skin that envelops is itself only the development and putting into play, the general exposition, of the whole circumscribing of the body (of all its detachment). *Ex-peau-sition* is possible to say, playing with the French. In German, one could play on *Aus-sein/Haut-sein*; in English, *ex-skin-bition*.

But in every language the important thing is that the exposition, the *Ausstellen* (exhibition) that is the body and its *Ausdehnen/extension* (*Psyche ist ausgedehnt*, "Psyche is extended," wrote Freud) does not consist of a fixed display (*étalement*) like the picture rail of an art gallery. On the contrary, this exhibition is understood only as constant movement, undulation, deployment, and re-ployment, an ever-changing pace (*allure*) in contact with all other bodies—which is to say, in contact with everything that approaches and with everything one approaches.

As we have known since Aristotle, the identity of the perceptible (*sensible*) and of the sentient in sensing (*le sentir*) (which is also a being-sensed, *un être-senti*), itself similar to the identity of the thinkable and the thinker in the act of thinking, implies for the point of sensation—in vision, hearing, smelling, tasting and touch—a way of co-penetration of both in the act and as this act. The sensitive act, that is, according to the Aristotelian concept of act—*Energeia*—forms the actual effectiveness, the event that is produced from sensation. The soul that senses is itself sensitive (*sensible*, perceptible) and because of this senses itself sensing (*se sent sentir*). Nowhere is this clearer—nowhere more perceptible (*sensible*)—than in touch: Neither eye, nor ear, nor nose, nor mouth feel themselves feeling with the intensity or precision of the skin. Image, sound, smell, taste remain in a way distinct from the sensing organ, even though they occupy it wholly. Probably the same is true for touch as soon as I imagine the substance touched (if I think "this cloth is rough," "this skin is cool"). But one can say, although it's actually impossible to determine these things, that representation is less immediate in touch. In the other senses, it announces itself more quickly, although in different ways according to the case (image is contemporaneous with its being seen; melody or timbre is likewise, if a little less so, with hearing; flavor even less with taste; and the odor is even more remote from olfaction, to the point of being on the same order as touch).[1]

This identity of touching and touched can only be understood as the identity of movement, motion and emotion. Precisely because it is not the identity of a representation or the thing it represents. The cool skin I speak of is not that first—"cool skin"—in the act of my hand touching it. But it "is" my gesture, it is my hand and my hand passes into it for my hand is in its contact or its caress (actually, no contact with skin—except medical contact—is exempt from the possibility of a caress). Motion and emotion—which really are a single thing—envelop the act, the *Energeia* of the senses. And this *Energeia* is nothing but the effectiveness of contact, which is the effectiveness of coming towards and of welcoming, a twofold quality that exchanges: I come toward the skin that welcomes me, my skin welcomes the coming which is for itself the welcome of the other. The coming-to of the two of them meets them at a point of semi-confusion. This point itself is not immobile: It is a "point" only as image; its reality is motion and emotion, stirring, traction and attraction, as well as uninterrupted variation, fluctuation. It is at the same time vibration, palpitation of one against the other, swaying of one with the other, and for that reason "identity" is not identical with itself even though it gathers both and shares both presences in a shared coming (*venue*).

That is the *rühren* of touch. Fluid movement of a rhythm, wave swell, backwash of ex-istence which is "being outside" because the "outside" is the modulation, curve, and scansion of this floating and friction by which my body swims among all bodies and my skin alongside other skins.

So the movement of touch is not the one called by another term—*tasten* in German, *tâter* in French (or one could also use *palper*), *feel* or *palpate* in English—which could seem more appropriate. *Palpate* (tâter), in fact, is a cognitive, not affective, behavior. One palpates to recognize or evaluate a surface, a consistency, to estimate a density, a suppleness. But one does not caress in that way. Touch caresses, it is essentially caress, which is to say it is desire and pleasure of coming as close as possible to a skin—human, animal, textile, mineral, etc.—and using this proximity (that is, this superlative, extreme approach) to make skins play against each other.

This play renews the rhythm that is essentially and originally the play of inside/outside—the only play perhaps if all games consist of occupying and leaving positions, opening up distances, seizing and abandoning places, squares, periods. Touch is movement in that it is rhythmic, not a procedure or approach of exploration. "Approach" here does not mean coming into the vicinity, and "contact" does not mean establishing an exchange (of signs, signals, information, objects, services). Approach means extreme movement of closeness that will never be annulled into an identity, since "closest" has to remain distant, infinitesimally distant to be what it is. Contact means the shaking (*ébranlement*)—it too is superlative, extreme—of sensibility, that is, of the very thing that produces our capacity for receiving, for being touched. (*Rühren* can have the sense of playing an instrument, as in both French and English we used to speak of "touching the piano": It still means to awaken, to shake, animate.)

This play and this rhythm of touch are the *rühren* of a desire. Perhaps desire itself, since there is desire that does not desire to touch, if touch gives the pleasure of desire itself, the pleasure of desire striving toward closeness of relationship since relationship is nothing but putting into play the sharing of an inside and an outside.

The first and previously most widespread sense of *rühr* was that of sexual pleasure. The rhythmic movement and overflowing, the gushing that is not just of fluids but of whole bodies spreading out against each other, one into the other, and one moving away from the other only to resume and again put themselves together in the succession of waves that they become, each by the other: This movement does not belong to any process of action or cognition (we won't speak here of that finality that is procreation—which opens onto another body; for coming [*jouir*] is without finality or else has no other end than the one that suspends it above itself in the overflowing that exhausts it and opens it beyond itself).

We understand that the most widespread taboo relates to touch. Freud notes it, as ethnology and anthropology do. We are familiar with the importance of this taboo in our own culture: Although there isn't much ostensibly sacred about it, the taboo still supervises with jealous care all conditions, permissions, and modalities of the contact of bodies. We know precisely how far touch is permitted, even if it's just the other's hand, to say nothing of the rest of his or her body, and how far and in what way it is permissible to kiss, embrace, caress.

We know as a precise science how much touch engages being—and how, by consequence, being is strictly indissociable from relationship. There is not, absolutely not, "being" and then relationship. There is "being," the verb whose act and transitive nature are formed into relationship(s) and are only formed in that way. The "I am" of Descartes does not contravene this necessity any more than the "I" of Kant, Fichte, or Husserl, or the "*Jemein*" of Heidegger. Each "I" is, and is nothing but, the act of its relating (*rapport*) striving toward the world—toward what we call "the other," whose alterity is revealed in touch or as touch.

Touch—which with nothing random about it has given its name to a mode of divine intervention in the soul—as motion and emotion of the other consists at once of the point of a contact and of the reception or acceptance of its pressure and its reception. It brushes against and pricks, pierces, or grasps, indiscernibly and in a vibration from which it immediately withdraws. It is already itself its own trace, that is, it erases itself as mark, isolated imprint, while propagating the effects of its motion and emotion.

Saint John of the Cross speaks of "touches of union serving to unite passively the soul to God" and he goes on to say "the understanding must do nothing in connection with these feelings, but must conduct itself passively, and not interfere by applying to them its natural capacity. For [. . .] the understanding, with its activity, would very easily disturb and ruin the effect of these delicate manifestations of knowledge, which are a delectable supernatural intelligence that human nature cannot attain or apprehend by its own efforts, but only by remaining in a state of receptivity."[2] Not "understanding actively" is understanding passively; it is tasting a flavor, feeling a touch. The mystic does not have a monopoly over this metaphor—if there is one. The "touch" of a painter, the "touch" of a pianist (and the "*touches*" [keys] of the piano, and why not that of a computer keyboard), the "touch" one can add ("of whimsy," "of melancholy," and so on) to a setting or a text as well as the erotic "touch"[3] share the same quality, at once isolated and vibratory.

But it's never a matter of metaphor. It's always a matter of a perceptible, material, hence vibratory, reality. When the soul trembles, it truly trembles, just like water close to the boiling point. What we call "soul" nowadays is actually nothing but the awakening and welcoming—both intermingled—of motion/emotion. The soul is the body touched, vibrant, receptive, responding. Its response is the sharing of touch, its rising up to it. It rises up, *se soulève*, as the German *Aufruhr* says, which designates, as I've remarked, social or political uprising. There is insurrection, in fact—and sometimes erection—in the motion of touch. A body rebels against its own closure, against its being enclosed in itself, against its entropy. It rebels against its death. Perhaps it's not impossible that the very touch of death sets off a final uprising (*surrection*), destruction and abandon at the same time.

Whether it's a question of the coming of an other, or the absolute alteration of death, it's the body that opens up and extends itself to the outside. That is its pure act: Just as Aristotle's Prime Mover is pure *Energeia* in which no "power" (*dunamis*, potentiality) remains. That is to say there is nothing to wait for, nothing that can come from outside, so when I am *touched* I have nothing to wait for: The touch is everything in action, in its mobile, vibratory, sudden action. And just as for Aristotle's god, this action is accompanied by its own excess, which is its *jouissance*, the pleasure that is the flower or brilliance of the action—sun or darkness, always an abyss toward which spreads or gushes the *rühr* of *berühren*.

—Vienna, Tanzquartier, 2010

Neither Seeing Nor Having
(Ni le voir ni l'avoir)

1

At the end of Canto V of his poem, Dante faints: "I fainted, and, as if I were dying, fell, as a dead body falls."[1] Gérard Granel wrote about the poem and left an unfinished text, a first draft of which *Poésie* published in 2001 "out of fidelity to the work of Granel" whose life a "mortal illness" cut short.

Granel disappeared in the disappearance[2] of Dante and with it. The fainting of the poet does not appear in the philosopher's text, although nothing stops us from imagining that Granel would have elaborated and commented on this episode. Nothing prevents us, for death does not prevent us from "superimposing the past over the interminable" as Granel wrote at the beginning of the text he devoted to the great book by Reiner Schürmann, a text he published after Schürmann's death.

Everything is posthumous here, everything past, and everything returns and is pursued, not by brilliant paradox or by dialectical ingenuity, but by the effect of this "essential formality of our being in each person,"[3] which entrusts us with "the task of dying,"[4] which could well be that of not "going anywhere"[5]—or else of "going nowhere," as he prefers to say: This question of how to say it is one that should concern us to conclude, or not to conclude it, yet not give ourselves over to the "perpetual return of the *over-plus* [. . .] and of the limitless."[6]

2

Nowhere, we will see, is the true place of the *archai* named by our text (*Un désir d'enfer*, "A Desire of Hell"), and hence of every kind of *archi-* anything. It is also the place where the "event" can occur previous to any "form" of an *"epiphaneia"* whose name and description I borrow from Alessandro Trevini: the one "that each person can feel for an instant and through which is also targeted the other-than-me."[7] It is, in fact, to a couple and even a coupling that Granel confides the revelation of a passage toward the "nowhere" where *jouissance*, its desire, and the fainting of the one who expresses them are mingled indistinctly. Who expresses them and who experiences them, who, by expressing them, experiences them.

This couple is not one in which the "symbolic hunger divides in order to satisfy itself," the hunger present "in the heart of power itself" and which forms "the irresistible impulse to see oneself in its mirror," the impulse conveyed by "the profound identity of Faust and Marguerite" as Granel evokes it in discussing "form-colloquium" in 1992.[8]

Trying to be faithful while not gazing at each other, then, or at ourselves in Granel, let us move away from the damnation of Faust to move toward that other damnation from which its own poet causes to emerge, during the narrative time, an entirely other couple whose episode Granel takes up to recite, re-speak, its event and desire.

It is while listening to Francesca da Ramini retell her loving embrace that Dante faints, and it is the story of Francesca and Paolo as Dante sings it to us that offers Granel the opportunity for a superb variation on the subject of desire—and not just "on the subject of" since this variation is itself lifted, carried by *the one* desire that turns out to be its *subject* in every possible way and especially as the philosopher-subject who faints.

3

The subject-desire of speech or of the text—probably there's not much difference between the two,[9] especially in Granel whose writing often likes to manifest as speech (through questions, exclamations, the use of the "I" and the "you," syncopes and caesuras, and so on)—this desire is "of Hell" (that is the title of the text) first of all because in Dante it is condemned to Hell because of the sin of adultery. But what Granel wants to extract from it is the threefold determination of desire that must in every sense be called *impeccable*: desire emerging from Hell, desire offered by Hell, and above all desire that proceeds at the pace of Hell in accordance with that figure of speech that uses *infernal* to express a feverish, rushed speed, a frantic rhythm—in short, desire carrying one away.

This desire can open the mouth to a poem and to the kiss of wild love, but it can also get carried away like the mad quest for infinite production of wealth marching the producer to an infernal rhythm.

Between each desire, between each madness, the most profound difference is the following: Eros knows it "does not go anywhere" as Granel says here, whereas Production pursues a goal that is at once precisely projected and indefinitely renewed according to "the law of increasing capitalization of real capital,"[10] which constitutes "capital itself" as the non-apparent "form" of this law.

The difference, in other words, is between a nonknowing in the heart of the "production of *jouissance*"— to speak like Trevini—and a knowing elaborated from the process of market production. But it should be pointed out: On one hand non-knowing recognizes itself as such, and consists of fainting; on the other, knowledge claims to know not only about productive and accumulative processes but also about knowledge itself (science of science as supposed knowledge of the object) *and* at the same time knowledge of desire as desire, it too, of object and *jouissance* as object and objective satisfaction (hence sex can be produced and consumed but perhaps not written in the conjoined fainting of a poet and a thinker).

4

Before going any further we understand that it's not chance or some passing whim that Granel devotes a text to desire. On the contrary, an imperious necessity is at stake: that of approaching the suspension of power (*pouvoir*) along with that of knowing (*savoir*), of having and of seeing (*de l'avoir et du voir*).

The text breaks off—since it is unfinished—at sentences that pronounce "*the being-displayed as such (tireless promenade where desire advances, without going anywhere)*" and announces the possibility of "*breaking all the obvious statements in discourse on body and soul, love,* identity" in favor of the non-conceptual (*horsconcept*) affirmation according to which "*something connects [. . .] a shoulder joint, a distribution of colors, an algebraic formula, like so many fragments of 'The Thing', like so many forms of existential formality.*"[11]

"Something connects" the "fragments of the Thing," something that must be the thing of the thing and must stem, to do this, from that "nowhere" where desire promenades itself. But "existential formality" is indeed the same as the already-cited "essential formality of our being" because the essence here is none other than existence precisely as *form* in the sense that Granel strives to convey it, that is, in the sense of the non-apparent formation of all appearing forms, of all discernible conformations and configurations.

The "task of dying," because that is what characterizes essential formality, must then be understood with the stress placed on *task*, as much for our being in the singular as for our plural "being together," as the quoted text also says.

The task is not a labor, especially not a productive labor, at least not one productive of objects.[12] The task does not produce, it attempts, it tries, not without difficulty—"so laboriously that following it is truly 'a hell'"[13]—a hell into which one descends thanks to a remembering that is not a conserving, but the "cruel"[14] reopening of a mouth charged with the task of expressing desire. Thus, and we will return to this, Granel again opens the book and the mouth of Dante.

Is this task linked to that of dying? Isn't it a question, here as well as there, of a similar "fainting grasp"[15] (*saisie évanouissante*)—that is, of nothing that one can take hold of as a product or that one can enjoy as a property. If it is a question of producing, it is so in the sense of carrying forward, and if it is a question of enjoying, it is while being carried even further forward. If it is a question finally of dying, then it is in Blanchot's sense of "dying," rather than of death.

5

The task here demands the "courage" of "examining the trait of a retreat."[16] Of acknowledging *that*—and possibly how, but not "why" because there is no reason—it is arriving, it is coming, it is "advancing." For desire does nothing but advance and while advancing makes itself "revealed" (*à découvert*),[17] exposed, that is, ex-isting, being there.

Dying, then, not by ceasing to live but by experiencing the "fainting grasp"—an expression by which, we should have no doubt, Granel was preparing what he did not get to write: the passage where Dante faints, "falling like a dead man" as he himself describes it. Fainting or "relinquishing" grasp Granel says in discussing Schürmann, evoking "the consent of the thinker to 'relinquishing' [*dessaisie*] as the only attitude that suits the dereliction in which modern humanity finds itself plunged."[18]

Everything occurs, from one text to the other, between texts—Granel's and Dante's, or else, as we'll see, the one by Dante and the one by an unnamed author; everything occurs as the co-presence or competition of two relinquishings, as their ultra-thin joining. The dereliction of "modern humanity" *or* the exposure to that which exceeds any grasp and any control. The fate of the damned of the earth *or* the fate of those damned to a hell that is nonetheless in heaven.

Granel titles his text "A Desire of Hell" to convey what he calls here "Caesura of Fate itself,"[19] which he likens to the scansion of the Latin pair "*Fas / Nefas*" about which we are not allowed to forget that it's a question here of what is said (*fari*) and more precisely of "speech as independent of the one uttering it and not as it signifies but as it exists."[20]

"Caesura of Fate" means that fate carries caesura, its own caesura. That it is caesura. This means it leads desire where it goes—to the "nowhere" of a darkness that will turn out to be *body*: for one arrives at the body by the movement and impetus of a text that signals toward it without signifying it. The story of a kiss *gives rise to* or *provokes* the lovers' kiss. It *produces* this kiss by *provocation*, it *summons* it and falls silent to open itself to it. Caesura forms the disjunctive joining of text and body, the two "roots" of Eros, says Granel, by taking up the word that Dante places in Francesca's mouth.

6

According to the hypothesis I'm forming in trying to extend the unfinished text, when desire does not reach the caesura that disconnects a sense (the sense of desire) and the senses (also of desire: trembling, kiss, fainting), the same desire—the same altered—carries onward from hell toward another damnation in which without caesura, according solely to the law of a "tireless"[21] progression becoming uniform, it gives itself over to the "limitless self-increasing" whose name for Granel is "power" (*pouvoir*),[22] whose reality is "production," and whose meaning or form is the "spirit of wealth"[23] or else the "growth of nonexistence,"[24] which is also "political nonexistence"[25] in the sense—to which we will return—of the "arch-political."

Where nonexistence increases, there is manifested the "primitiveness" of existing.[26] That is, an "Arch-phenomenon"[27] or an inaugural "Form," a forming form, the *mise-en-forme* of the act of existing or the "existential formality" that precedes, defies, and "ruptures discourses about body and soul, love, identity" as we have already read.[28]

This primitive formation will have begun in a desire, that of Greek nudity[29] that manifests as desire as harmony of proportions. This desire has allowed itself to be converted to the figurative rhythm with its infinitesimal calculus[30] and thus to the literally disproportionate culture "of power over the world."[31]

What is at stake for Granel as well as for us is what Alessandro Trevini calls "the *active suspension* of forms serving as a vehicle for excessiveness,"[32] or a way of "experiencing differently" a "measure" of "*jouissance*" unique to each person. It seems to me that it's something along these lines that Granel makes us glimpse with his desire of hell.

Desire syncopated by its own caesura, or infinite search for a self-increasing, forms two ways of touching the *archi* or *archai* as our text says[33]—a text in which, we should note in passing, Granel for once retains the *archi-* in his closure, which he calls "metaphysical." I quote: "Archi-caesura, we might immediately be tempted to translate, incurable metaphysicians that we are."[34] He has just spoken of the "caesura of Fate itself" as the one that is at play where it is a question of "saying what does not want to be said"—or formation previous to any formed form.

So there is an essential ambiguity, and with it an essential fragility of this prefix—*archi*—that is permanently in flux.

7

There are two domains of *archai*. That of the Moderns and of "Apodicticity," here likened to "Informatics,"[35] that is, the irrevocable necessity of immediately available information, all memory stored. To this *archè* one does not revert back: It is there, at hand. At bottom it is nothing but the *archè* of rulership, not of beginning.[36]

The other demands a descent into its profundity that is even longer—by right interminable—because what it seeks has never been in action—"even though," and I quote the text, "it's a matter of a 'passage to action': love, the kiss on the mouth"[37]—never in action, then, without being potential (*en puissance*), pending, or virtual, like a pre-formed model. It is a question of what "only the story" is leading us toward, since the story—speech, the mouth, the very mouth that has kissed, that kisses the caesura of itself as speaker—speech, then, "launches [*déclenche*]."[38] It launches by telling about the kiss. Once again, it provokes it, and the "passage to action" is not the actualization of a potential but the response to a summons, the silent resounding of the text.

Desire is moved by speech but not by any evocation that might suggest an imitation. This is the crucial point, the point where caesura plays its decisive role, as this unfinished text does not explain to us but asks us to understand. What the kiss produces is not an imaginary evocation that would lead to mimicry. It is in a way, on the contrary, the arising of the discrepancy and contrast between the words and the reality they name: The story of the kiss opens into—and is suspended within—the "opacity" of bodies, as the text says.[39] The discrepancy arises between the signification noted as "kiss" and the kiss of mouths lips to lips. In this discrepancy, "the lovers topple over"[40] and become lovers—without it actually being possible to determine if they were already lovers "before" or only "after." The time of the *archè* is an immemorial present, always-already come and never-yet arrived. It is a production that is always-already produced and never-yet consummated/consumed as product.[41]

The *archè* is at play here in the caesura that joins and disjoins in the same suspense the sense spoken by the mouth and the sensation experienced by that same mouth. The kissing lips interrupt the course of the voice by doing what the voice says, but the voice, by saying, itself does nothing other than indicate the interruption of its course, the necessity that it no longer have currency (*qu'elle n'ait plus cours*).

This twofold movement by which story and kiss refer to each other on either side of their caesura, Granel designates—taking up the word used by Dante's Francesca—as "the two roots" [42] of desire. The first is the body in its "opacity," [43] the second is speech, story, or text by which opacity (in itself withdrawn from the body) is designated as withdrawn. By the story in fact. By the story of the kiss and its caesura from the kiss itself, we are permitted "to know that one can neither see it nor have it." [44]

This lesson—for it is one, it is the "Knowledge" that is "neither science, nor wisdom, nor religion," [45] "but furnace [. . .] where these three are fused," [46] consequently knowledge of hell—this lesson is given, Granel emphasizes twice, within the framework or on the stage of Dante's poem and in it of a "story within the story," that is, of a theatricality whose artifice of "*mise en présence*" [47] "caesuras the massiveness" of presence.

Mise en scène (staging), as *mise en récit* (telling) and *mise en bouche* (using the mouth, kissing), caesuras compact opacity, opens it up and closes it again in the kiss. Remember the whole arrangement (the entirety of which Granel does not give in the text he has left us): Francesca tells Dante how Paolo and she were reading about the love affairs of Lancelot and Guinevere, for whom Galahad, Arthur's seneschal, arranged an adulterous tryst. Francesca explains how this reading was to them identical to the machination of the seneschal and like him played the "launcher" (*déclencheur*)[48] of the love deed.

"The book and its author" says Francesca in the words Dante gives her—the book and its author were for us Galahad, the "procurer." And the poet faints at this story whose author he is, and Granel explains to us how his own reading, which through him becomes ours, opens inside our body what we cannot see or have, but only know with that knowledge that makes Granel himself burn from pleasure.

8

But this pleasure touches on nothing else—one might risk saying: kisses nothing else—with the body than "a significant expression of the very possibility of existing."[49] What the next page—suspense of the interrupted text—will call "existential formality." It is the *mise en présence* of the body as that "material apriori"[50] of Husserl reformulated into "logical matter" by Granel, or else that "pure ontological space"[51] where one can certainly recognize the *da* of *Dasein* but returned to its most characteristic formal primitivity.

So the text we are reading teaches us that desire moves toward that *archè* of the "possibility of existing," to that point—neither material nor spiritual—where sense is suspended while opening and closing (by the same caesura) its saying and its un-saying (*son dire et son dé-dire*), or even its delirium (*son délire*). And that is what there is no question of seeing or having.

Seeing and having, on the contrary, hence also knowing and foreseeing, having in an infinite multiplying, this is the self-productive logic that ignores caesura and body as suspense of sense. It is the production of product in the limitless reproduction of wealth.

Wealth forms ideally whatever can be seen and had. That which can be known with a knowledge in which another hell rumbles, that of the damned of the Earth— both rich and poor—who are not the condemned ones of desire. In this they resemble one another in that they "are going nowhere." On one hand, nowhere gives itself over to accumulation itself; on the other, it gives itself over to caesura where desire is suspended along with sense.

Similarly, it is possible to say that the two *archai* resemble each other—just as in this text, digital memory and unstable memory resemble each other, one perpetually present, the other striving toward the *mise en présence* of that which, by its very essence, escapes.

What is common to both *archai* is nothing other than their essential difference from that in respect to which they are *archè*. Granel phrased it this way: "An 'archi' has nothing to do with what it is the archi of, whereas what it commands has everything to do with it."[52] Thus, "Capital itself" as "law of increasing capitalization" is "fundamentally indifferent" to "real capital."[53]

Similarly, "Caesura" is foreign to the mouth that speaks it as well as to the mouth that kisses it. But just as real capital obeys the formality of capitalization, so do words and kisses respond to their common disjunction.

An *archi-politics* has nothing to do with politics, then. On the contrary, it is impelled by the "quest for the Primitive" as a " 'we all' previous to each of us."[54] In a similar way, an *archi-erotics* has nothing to do with the erotic. On the contrary, it is impelled by the desire that "scrutinizes with its gaze," "the trait of retreat"[55] of that body it takes from the other, from whom it takes "la bella persona" as Dante says in a way that Granel calls "astounding"[56] because Francesca finds herself stripped of herself.

But doesn't this parallel also suggest an indication toward a crossing of one *archi* with the other? Isn't it on the side of a "we" previous to each person that something could be at play—if not "the Thing" itself—of the mouths joined between story and kiss? And isn't it on the side of desire that there should advance, "without going anywhere," what Granel has phrased as "the uplift of a 'sense of Being' *who* gives itself a humanity (not *that* a humanity gives itself)—this time 'our own'"?[57]

This rush of chiasmus is not resolved, however, in an equivalence. To the two *archai* belongs also an arch-difference that holds them at a distance. A caesura that does not allow the reabsorption into a principle. A principle-ness more archaic than any principle or any origin, a plurality in *archi*.

Isn't it necessary, in fact, that "politics take Difference as its as 'object' and 'aim'"?[58] By that we understand an arch-politics and consequently, too, a task guided by the differences between politics and erotics as well as between erotics and aesthetics, or even between poetics and mathematics, and so on. But still at the same time between one hell and another, one furnace and another, the consumption of a product and the desire of a mouth.

9

Coda

A few years before the unfinished "A Desire of Hell," in one of the *Études* collected in 1995, "Le monde et son expression" ("The World and Its Expression"), Gérard Granel had made the woman's body into the symbol for the world, thus clearing the way that Dante enlarges. That which for the poet took the shape of the kiss presented itself rather as a denuding—another aspect of the same astonishment (*saisissement*).

Granel speaks of modesty about which, he says, "the most modest desire has always been to be known: not forced, but so to speak convinced little by little (like an incredulity that incredibly demolishes itself) of finally having found the eyes that will not tire of looking at how much—and in how many thousands of ways—one *cannot* see (possess) it. The 'female nude' proliferates in painting only because the body of women is, under this aspect, the symbol of the world."

So we can better re-read the phrase in the "Desire of Hell": "To discover in the body what painting discovers in the world, namely that one can neither see it, nor have it." We see, in fact, more clearly, in the brilliance of shamelessness, how what is at stake is a gaze that sees without having and thus without seeing, that sees the beyond-visible (*outre-visible*) of both the text (of the poem), and of painting—but also how what is impossible either to see *it* or *her* (*ne de* le *voir ni de* la *voir*) is "woman" and at the same time "world" only because it does not allow itself to be assigned a single gender and on the contrary hovers between "*le*" and "*la*," between Paolo and Francesca, like the open book that falls from their hands.

—*Jean Luc Nancy*

As I finished the preceding pages, Élisabeth Rigal, who knew their title, pointed out to me the passage in Granel's *Études*. Pierre-Philippe Jandin did the same two days later. Granel's *continuo* could not go unperceived.

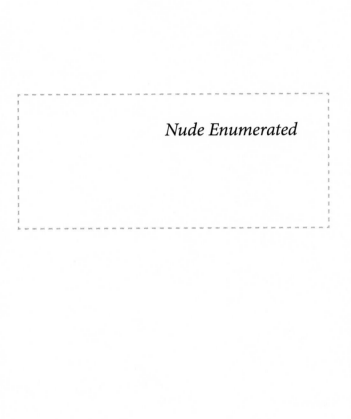

Nude Enumerated

Nude: conquered, triumphant; undone, reassembled; lost, found; undressed, costumed; obvious, indiscernible; shameless, virtuous; sexed, neutralized.

Nude knot tied up in contradictions. Not dialectical for all that. No mediation between naked dearth of hair and the luxuriance of tufts. No middle way or replacement or surpassing. But rather contradictory joinings. Fragile sturdy; smooth rough; dry wet; empty full; open closed.

It gets stuck, a little. Clashes, argues, plays with the other. Challenges, mistrusts, slips and slides. Each body body-to-body with its nude.

Its own nude—but actually, not its own. Neither improper nor unclean (at first). Something else. Its most proper impropriety.

Me there not me ever. Not this hair not this mark not this wart not this wrinkle. How to say I'm naked without saying another he/she. The nude sweats with you and to you. Your buttock is no longer yours. Was it ever? Was it nude without being felt?

Nude through the slit in clothes. This only obeys that: One dresses in order to strip bare. Nudity must appear. It is not simply present: It can seem or remain veiled. Veiled it asserts its unveiling. The size, nature and justification of the veil are matters of culture. Here one wears a penis sheath, there a plunging neckline, here one goes out in shorts and there in long tunics; one covers the mouth, the hair, the sex, the leg. One uncovers the thigh, the navel, the shoulder or only the eyes.

The nude body hides some places in itself. The anus is not apparent, or the perineum. The orifices let a little, a very little, of their mysteries be glimpsed.

Nude contained, not occurring (*contenu, non advenu*). Unrecognized (*Méconnu*). Well-come or ill-come according to how one uses it.

For nudity offers its use: To do this it has lips, folds, meatuses, cleavages, hollows, leaks.

It has schemes of skin—rough, taut, hairy, fine, sleek. It has ways of showing itself and blinding at the same time. Inside one sees nothing with the eyes.

Eyes nose, fingers tongue inside.

The tongue in the nude lacks language. Lack of decent words, for decency is silent. Says ass, pussy or else cock, prick or dick. Says it fast and withdraws itself grunting.

Inside is it still naked or else really raw? Rawness of nudity: becomes flesh and heat, becomes something pampered rushing to the ever-more-hidden depths.

Nude turns round and curls up like a glove, a slip, a reel. Nude turned over is no longer nude but confused, moist and indistinct. The skin rubs against itself, against you. You are mingled at every approach.

Naked bodies make each other sweat, they come in a sweat. Make themselves suckers and savors, smells, salts, salivas, solutions. Wet bodies irrigated liquefied distilled. Aqua-vitas with their acid fruits.

Light nude disposed to dissipate, naked clouds (*nuées*) floating at the whim of the winds. Their breaths gather them press them, mix them untangle them, stretch them out draw them back.

Easy nude once known but never recognized always difficult. Always fleeing and furtive. Always resuming itself reserving itself to become more nude and better nude. Overwhelming the singular you, demanding the plural you: the holding back, the slow-to-come. Demanding prudent ardor and thoughtful modesty.

Nudity disappears in medical undressing. Becomes ingenuousness, haecceity and fortuity. Nude stripped bare. Nude inspected: map, number, system and dia-stema. Metabolism without hyperbole.

Is therefore no longer nude but dressed with—metria (anthropo-bio-therapo).

At the police station nude filed away clothed with fingerprints clues suspected of concealment.

Never nude, then, unless without equipment, without calm and without observer.

Unobservable obscenizable. Desire alone knows how to contemplate, desire of lover desire of artist the desire of the engorger, desire of elsewhere.

Always elsewhere the male/female nude: not here, which welcomes only clothed people, but over there somewhere undecided at a distance within reach of de-sire of touching flattering hiding staining.

Once gods animals vegetables minerals: dressed in leaves bark flowers seeds or else furs shells scales and feathers teguments. Not much later, we ourselves with huge phallus huge vulva.

Became naked. Perfect men, women perfect. Apollo-nian, Venusian forms.

The gods were born—that means: the nudes are gods the nudes goddesses. Divine is nude and the divine nude.

Divine is nude: a little like death. Divine nude: as if forever immortal.

*   *   *

Being reborn at each birth. Nude as a worm: without hair or shell, just covered with slime (*glaire*). It will end up glory, anamorphosis of the same vitreous substance, of the lucid skin where all nudity is wrapped.

Rauba was the word for booty, what one robs from the enemy, despoiling, skinning, undressing him. The naked woman, man: the enemy undressed.

Always the nude concealed, deprived of clothes and access. Touching it moves it further away. Nudity renews, regenerates, revives itself.

Makes itself another world, opens up universe, pluriverse, obverse and reverse, belly and rump, shoulder and neck, lobes and loins, hollow of back, cleavage, cleft, bird's nest, comet tail, ring and black hole, milky way O luminous sister, stories of long thighs, excitement of alcoves, cultures, pearls and henna, sonorous jewels, myths, combinings, ephemeral movements, sweats, blushes,

tastes,

pallors.

NOTES

FROM ANIMAL INSTINCT TO DESIRE OF THE OTHER: HOW TO GO FROM *PLAISIR* TO *JOUIR*?

1. Henri Focillon, *The Life of Forms in Art,* trans. Charles B. Hogan and George Kubler (New York: Zone Books, 1992), 34.

2. *Quelqu'un qui n'est pas "canon": canon* can mean a cannon literally or, more idiomatically, it can mean someone is gorgeous, handsome.—Trans.

3. *Souffrance* can mean "suffering," but it can also mean something that's pending—*en souffrance* means pending, in transit.—Trans.

TOWARD INFINITY AND BEYOND: IS THERE AN ART TO *JOUIR*?

1. Henry Miller, *Sexus: The Rosy Crucifixion* (New York: Grove Press, 1994), 57–58.

2. *Faire* in slang can mean to screw someone.—Trans.

3. Rainer Maria Rilke, *Letters to a Young Poet*, trans. M. D. Herter Norton (New York: Norton, 1993), 24.

4. "I come and go, between your loins, and I hold myself back . . ."—Trans.

5. *Zoner* can mean to hang around, to linger.—Trans.

THE CONDEMNATION OF *JOUISSANCE*

1. Li Yu, *Jou Pu Tuan (The Prayer Mat of Flesh)* (New York: Grove Press, 1967).

FROM PROFIT TO CONSUMPTION/CONSUMMATION: CAN WE ENJOY EVERYTHING?

1. Albert Camus, *The Myth of Sisyphus and Other Essays*, trans. Justin O'Brien (New York: Vintage, 1991), 153.

2. The French translation is different from the published English translation; I have translated the French literally here. For a comparison, see "The First Element: The Idea of God In and For Itself" on page 417 ff. of Hegel's *Lectures on the Philosophy of Religion: The Lectures of 1827*, ed. Peter C. Hodgson (Oxford: Oxford University Press, 2006).

3. Immanuel Kant, *Anthropology from a Pragmatic Point of View*, ed. Robert B. Louden (Cambridge: Cambridge University Press, 2006), 128.

RÜHREN, BERÜHREN, AUFRUHR (MOVING, TOUCHING, UPRISING)

1. It is impossible for me to linger over this in the framework of this lecture, but we should refine the differential analysis of the senses. They all participate in touch in that they all bear the possibility of the identity of sensing and sensed. But each one modulates in its own way this identity and the difference of modulations is inherent to sensibility, which cannot be single or general. If it were, it would only have an abstract "sensibility," a concept of sensibility. But in each domain it brings forward (*fait valoir*) both a sense (visual, auditory, etc.) *and* the plurality of senses, that is, the fact that they refer to each other in differential, inexhaustible ways. One can also conceive them all under the model of touch *and* differentiate them all by relating one to another of them. But—and to say no more about it—taste and smell engage the inside/outside relationship differently: For them there is absorption, assimilation of a very particular order. What's more, taste concerns especially a consistent sensation, solid or liquid; smell an evanescent, gaseous, aerial sensation. Each time the

relationship differs with the extent and movement unique to touch. Each time it is a matter of special *touches*, whose significance varies from one body to another: One person might "have a nose" as they say, or another might "have an ear" . . . This "have" is a way of touching / being touched.

2. From Chapter 32 of *The Essential St. John of the Cross*.

3. In French and English, "touch me," "you touch yourself," taken absolutely, are erotic statements.

NEITHER SEEING NOR HAVING (*NI LE VOIR NI L'AVOIR*)

1. Canto V of Dante's *Inferno*, online: http://www .poetryintranslation.com/PITBR/Italian/DantInf1to7 .htm#anchor_Toc64090929.

2. In French, "disappearance," *la disparition*, often is used for death.—Trans.

3. Gérard Granel, *Apolis* (Mauvezin, Editions T.E.R., 2009), 122.

4. Ibid.

5. Ibid., 147.

6. Ibid., 71. ("Over-plus" appears in English in the original; it is a reference to American capitalism.—Trans.)

7. Alessandro Trevini Bellini, *Suspension du capital-monde par la production de la jouissance* (doctoral thesis, Université Paris Ouest Nanterre, 2011), 623.

8. Granel, *Apolis*, 39.

9. If we need to pin it down, this affirmation is enough for Derrida, despite certain appearances in the Derrida canon.

10. Granel, *Apolis*, 75.

11. Ibid., 145–46.

12. Granel likes the word "task," whose essential extent for him one can find in a passage like this, where it is a question of "deciding again on the situation and inventing tasks for us (individually as well as in a group)," Gérard Granel, *L'époque dénouée* (Paris: Hermann, 2012), 34.

13. Granel, *Apolis*, 144.

14. Ibid.

15. Ibid. (A note on the phrase *saisie évanouissante*: *saisie*, from *saisir*, "to grasp," can mean seizure of property, confiscation of goods.—Trans.)

16. Ibid., 145.

17. Ibid.

18. Ibid., 134.

19. Ibid., 144. (The Latin *caesura* literally means "cutting." In prosody, it refers to the fluid breath pause or break in a metrical line. The French derivative *césure* is used [for instance by Philippe Lacoue-Labarthe in "The Caesura of the Speculative," as well as by Derrida] in the sense of break, rupture, deliberate gap, formal division, scission.—Trans.)

20. É. Benveniste, *Le Vocabulaire des institutions indo-européennes*, Vol. II (Paris: Minuit, 1969), 133.

21. Granel, *Apolis*, 145.

22. Ibid., 34.

23. For example, Ibid., 67.

24. Ibid., 101.

25. Ibid., 5.

26. Ibid., 80 and 5.

27. Ibid., 80.

28. Arché in Greek means "beginning or origin," the first. The root extends to forms meaning "first in the state," "ruler" (like the *archons* of Athens). The two flavors of the word are played with by Granel and Nancy; we in English observe the same duality (archeology is the discourse on beginnings, while an archbishop is a ruler of the clergy, and so on).—Trans.

29. Granel, *Apolis*, 81.

30. Ibid., 83.

31. Ibid.

32. Trevini Bellini, *Suspension du capital-monde*, 617.

33. Granel, *Apolis*, 144.

34. Ibid.

35. Ibid.

36. Rulership/beginning: *commandement, commencement.*—Trans.

37. Ibid.

38. Ibid., 145.

39. Ibid.

40. Ibid.

41. Perhaps this is what Alexandre Trevini calls "production of *jouissance.*"

42. Granel, *Apolis*, 145.

43. Ibid.

44. Ibid.

45. Ibid., 140.

46. Ibid., 140–41.

47. Ibid., 139, where the author of the text, Gérard Granel, suddenly and not without incongruity declares in his own text what pleasure he gets from the artifice of theater in general. In other words, he warns us about what he enjoys by delivering to us the lesson of the *archai* of desire.

48. Ibid., 145.

49. Ibid., 145.

50. Granel, *L'époque dénouée*, 47.

51. Granel, *Apolis*, 19.

52. Granel, *L'époque dénouée*, 41.

53. Granel, *Apolis*, 75.

54. Ibid., 5.

55. Ibid., 145.

56. Ibid., 143.

57. Ibid., 80.

58. Ibid., 58.

SOME BIBLIOGRAPHICAL
REFERENCE POINTS

Apollinaire, Guillaume. *Poèmes à Lou*. Paris: Gallimard, coll. "Poésie," 1969.

Saint Augustine. *Confessions*. Translated by Henry Chadwick. Oxford: Oxford University Press, 1991.

Bataille, Georges. *The Impossible*. Translated by Robert Hurley. San Francisco: City Lights, 2001.

Blanchot, Maurice. *The Inavowable Community*. Translated by Pierre Joris. Barrytown, New York: Station Hill Press, 1988.

Cummings, E. E. *Erotic Poems*. New York: Norton, 2010.

Duras, Marguerite. *The Malady of Death*. Translated by Barbara Bray. New York: Grove Press, 1986.

Focillon, Henri. *The Life of Forms in Art*. Translated by Charles B. Hogan and George Kubler. New York: Zone Books, 1989.

Freud, Sigmund. *Three Essays on the Theory of Sexuality*. Translated by James Strachey. Mansfield Centre, Conn.: Martino Fine Books, 2011.

Garrido, Jean-Manuel. *La Formation des formes*. Paris: Galilée, coll. "La philosophie en effet," 2008.

Jouve, Pierre Jean. "Les Beaux masques." In *Oeuvres II*. Paris: Mercure de France, 1987.

Kant, Immanuel. *Anthropology from a Pragmatic Point of View*. Edited by Robert B. Louden. Cambridge: Cambridge University Press, 2006.

———. *Critique of Pure Reason*. Translated by Marcus Weigelt. London and New York: Penguin Books, 2007.

Lacan, Jacques. *The Seminar of Jacques Lacan: On Feminine Sexuality, the Limits of Love and Knowledge* (Encore, Book XX). Edited by Jacques-Alain Miller. Translated by Bruce Fink. New York: Norton, 1999.

Lévi-Strauss, Claude. *Tristes Tropiques*. Translated by John and Doreen Weightman. New York: Penguin Books, 2012.

Li, Yu. *Jou Pu Tuan (The Prayer Mat of Flesh)*. New York: Grove Press, 1967.

Miller, Henry. *Sexus: The Rosy Crucifixion*. New York: Grove Press, 1994.

Plato. *Phaedrus*. Translated by Alexander Nehamas and Paul Woodruff. Indianapolis: Hackett, 1995.

Rilke, Rainer Maria. *Letters to a Young Poet*. Translated by M. D. Herter Norton. New York: Norton, 1993.

de Sade, Marquis. *Philosophy in the Boudoir: Or, The Immoral Mentors.* Translated by Joachim Neugroschel. New York: Penguin Classics, 2006.

de Spinoza, Benedict. *Ethics.* Translated by Edwin Curley. New York: Penguin Classics, 2005.

Zaloszyc, Armand. *Freud et l'énigme de la jouissance.* Toulon, France: Editions du Losange, 2009.